Joe Dogs

The Life & Crimes of a Mobster

by **Joseph "Joe Dogs" Iannuzzi**

SIMON & SCHUSTER

New York   **London**   **Toronto**   **Sydney**   **Tokyo**   **Singapore**

SIMON & SCHUSTER
Simon & Schuster Building
Rockefeller Center
1230 Avenue of the Americas
New York, New York 10020

SIMON & SCHUSTER and colophon are registered trademarks
of Simon & Schuster Inc.

Designed by Levavi & Levavi
Manufactured in the United States of America

10 9 8 7 6 5 4 3 2 1

Library of Congress Cataloging-in-Publication Data
Iannuzzi, Joseph.
    Joe Dogs : the life and crimes of a mobster / by Joseph "Joe Dogs"
Iannuzzi.
    p. cm.
    1. Iannuzzi, Joseph.   2. Mafia—United States—
Biography.   3. Criminals—United States—Biography.   I. Title.
HV6446.I18   1993
364.1′092—dc20
[B]   93-19991
                                                                     CIP

ISBN: 0-671-79752-2

The names of some individuals have been changed.

For Francie

The Players

THE GAMBINO *FAMIGLIA*

Carlo "Don Carlo" Gambino Boss of the Gambino Family, the nation's most powerful Mafia Family, until his death in 1976

Paul "Big Paulie" Castellano Succeeded Carlo Gambino as boss in 1976; held position until murdered in 1985

Joseph N. Gallo Longtime *consigliere* of Gambino Family; archenemy of Joe "Joe Dogs" Iannuzzi

Aniello "Neil" Dellacroce mentor of John Gotti, rival of Paul Castellano; Gambino Family underboss to both Carlo Gambino and Castellano

Joseph "Piney" Armone New York–based Gambino Family capo

Thomas "T.A." Agro Gambino Family soldier; member of Joe "Piney" Armone's crew; ran Southeast Florida for Gambino Family; Joe Iannuzzi's boss and mentor

Robert "Skinny Bobby" DeSimone
Louie Esposito
} Gambino Family associates; Florida–based members of Tommy Agro's crew

Paul Principe
Frank Russo
} Gambino Family associates; New York–based sluggers of Tommy Agro's crew

Andrew "Fat Andy" Ruggiano Miami–based Gambino Family capo

Gerald Alicino
Frank "Fingers" Abbandando
Salvatore Reale
Ronald "Stone" Pearlman
} Members of Fat Andy Ruggiano's crew

THE COLOMBO *FAMIGLIA*

Carmine "the Snake" Persico   Boss of the Colombo Crime Family

Gennaro "Gerry Lang" Langello   Colombo Crime Family under-boss

Dominic "Donny Shacks" Montemarano   Colombo Crime Family capo

Dominick "Little Dom" Cataldo   Colombo Crime Family soldier and hit man; sometime partner of Joe Iannuzzi

Ralphie ⎫ New York–based members of Little Dom Cataldo's
Billy Ray ⎭   crew

Nick "Jiggs" Forlano   Miami–based Colombo Family capo

John "Johnny Irish" Matera   Fort Lauderdale–based Colombo soldier who succeeded Jiggs Forlano as capo upon Forlano's death

Tony Black   Florida–based Colombo soldier

Thomas Farese   Fort Lauderdale–based Colombo soldier and drug dealer

Robert "Bobby Anthony" Amelia   Colombo Family associate; small-time drug dealer

Freddie "Freddie Campo" Campagnuolo   Palm Beach–based bookmaker and Colombo Family associate

Robbie   member of Freddie Campo Campagnuolo's crew

Prologue

WEST PALM BEACH, FLORIDA, MARCH 1981

"I got people that will eat the fucking eyes out of your fucking head! You dumb bastard! And they're as loyal as a motherfucker. With balls the size of cows. All I have to do is tell them to load up, be in this place at this time, and they'll walk in and blast everybody. No fuckin' hesitation. No nothin'. And don't look for nothin' beside it. No questions asked. They'll blow you up. You think you got something going? You got nothing going.

"You think I'm easy? You think I'm where I'm at today because I'm easy? What I've done you haven't dreamt of, my friend. Why do you think people fear me? Because I was a hard-on, you fuckin' moron? You think I got where I was because I was a jerkoff in the street? You're easy, you motherfucker. The most wrongest thing you ever did was fuck me. People fear me, you dumb fuck. You're only alive today, my friend, because Don's wife walked in. Not because we stopped. You wasn't supposed to walk away no more. And I'm gonna even enlighten you more better than that, while you're having these fuckin' hallucinations. I missed you three times. I was there looking for you two other times before this, you dumb motherfucker."

I lay in my bed holding the telephone receiver at arm's length, listening to Tommy Agro scream at the top of his lungs. My head ached. My broken ribs burned like kindling. And my nose, splayed across my face, was split down the middle. Attached to the telephone was a tape recorder, hooked up courtesy of the FBI office in West Palm Beach, Florida. It didn't take me long to get Tommy Agro to confess that he and two of his New York sluggers had flown to Palm Beach County to beat me to death. To make an example of me.

Two months earlier, on January 19, 1981, Tommy Agro had summoned me to Don Ritz's Pizzeria on Singer Island. He was there with two of his crew, Paul Principe and Frank Russo. They used lead pipes and a baseball bat, and the last thing I remember was Agro himself drawing back his leg and digging his dainty little alligator loafer deep into my ribs.

Tommy ran a crew for the Gambino Family, out of New York. He didn't usually leave jobs unfinished. I knew, because I was his right hand in Florida. But Don Ritz's wife walked in and spooked him just as he was about to chop off *my* right hand. Mafia symbolism.

So as Agro raged on, I smiled. Eight weeks later it still hurt to smile through my swollen face, but I couldn't help it. His verbal rampage lasted a good fifteen minutes. I had one thought: I've got him, and this will be the end. But it was only the beginning.

That tape ultimately was the start of an eighteen-month investigation that incarcerated—or made dead—a slew of wiseguys, lieutenants, capos, and bosses in the Gambino and Colombo Mafia Families from Miami to New York.

I'd awakened two days after the beating in St. Mary's Hospital. A priest. My mother and sister, who must have flown in from New York, told me he'd given me the last rites. Extreme Unction, my mother called it. My wife, Bunny, was there, and my girlfriend, Donna, standing next to one of my daughters. My first thought was What did I do? I didn't deserve this. Then I saw the feds back by the door. Special Agents Larry Doss and Gunnar Askeland of the FBI.

Tommy'd called that day, too. The first voice I'd heard coming out of a coma. "You'd better get me my money! Don't you get it in your dopey fuckin' head you're gonna disappear. You fucked up all Florida! Now you're where you belong. By yourself. Like a dog. I gave you the right name. Joe Dogs!" Pretty much the same rant he'd go on two months later. But I didn't have a tape recorder that day.

Jesus! I was angry. Not because of the unbelievable pain caused by the split nose, the busted ribs, or the grapefruit-sized hematoma on my temple. Not because my teeth had been knocked out and my

left ear partially severed. I was mad because my mentor, my close friend, my *compare,* did this to me because I was a lousy three months late on my juice payments. I was furious.

So I joined forces with the FBI, something that to this day I can't believe I did. I was forced to do it. I was a vegetable and I was in shock and I was to suffer from double vision for more than a year. And at first I hated myself for what I'd become.

But after a while, working with the feds, I started to enjoy myself. I was getting my revenge. On the Mafia. Nothing ever tasted as sweet.

Making
My
Bones

Night Raiders

"Joey, come here," my mother yelled. "Come and eat your oatmeal and get cleaned up. You're going with your father. It's Saturday."

I dropped whatever I was doing in the backyard of my parents' suburban two-family home in Port Chester, New York, and hurried into the house. I loved going with my dad on Saturdays, because everybody looked up to him. He was the local bookie. He was also in charge of the local numbers game, the "policy racket" they called it. Even in this little town twenty-five miles north of New York City there was plenty of action to be had.

We'd make the rounds of luncheonettes, restaurants, bars, even rich people's homes. And people would give me money because I was Joe Iannuzzi's kid. I remember going to a mansion and meeting the black guy who played Rochester in the old Jack Benny shows. I don't know if he lived there or worked there, but he gave me two silver dollars. He'd hit the number that day.

And then there was Tom Mix, the old movie cowboy. My dad would drive up to his ranch in Harrison, New York, a beautiful place. I posed for a picture with him, me sitting on a horse. He gave me a silver dollar, too. It was cowboys and Indians, because we

also had to stop by the local Indian reservation. They loved to bet. But they only gave me Indian head pennies.

My old man would take me to a restaurant and I got to eat anything I wanted. The people used to call him "Cheecha." I didn't know why they called him that. I was seven years old. And the apple hadn't fallen very far from the tree.

"Your grandmother had to bail you out, you bastard. You're just like your father, a no-good bum. You're making my life miserable." I had to take this from my mother. She had just sprung me from jail.

My first pinch. April 1945. I was fourteen years old. We had a gang. Called ourselves the "Night Raiders." We even had business cards printed. We'd break into a joint, rob it, and leave our cards, which read, "Compliments of the Night Raiders."

We were dumb kids making a living. My mother and father were divorced by then. Thank God. My old man would have broken my neck. My mother just yelled. About being embarrassed. "You're making it rotten for me and Eddie."

Eddie was the Irish guy she was dating. Later, after my father died, she married him. Eddie and I never got along. We'd have fistfights. I guess I was jealous because Eddie was going out with my mother and he treated my sisters better than he treated me.

"Fuck Eddie," I said to her. "I don't care how rotten I make it for that bum."

"Watch how you talk. You're going to be a gangster. Just like your father. He was a louse."

Then my mother shipped me off to live with my grandmother.

I went through the usual baloney a kid from a broken marriage goes through. Ran away from home, came back, ran away again. Finally I joined the army. That pleased my mother. I was now someone else's responsibility.

In the army I was disciplined. I had to take orders. It was the best thing that ever happened to me. I joined the boxing team and

learned to use my fists. I was decorated in Korea. I took a Chinese bayonet in the thigh. But once I received that honorable discharge I was right back out on the streets. Along the way I got married, had two little girls, got divorced, got married again, had another little girl, and settled down with a family—Sheryl, Debbie, Stephanie, and my wife, Bunny.

Well, I guess settling down isn't how most people would look at it.

Joe Diner

"Joey, did you do all the figuring on the bets for last week?"

"Yeah, Hook, here they are." It was 1966. I was thirty-five years old, living in Glen Cove, Long Island, and working in a diner. I was also connected to two bookmakers named Hook and Zabie. I never kidded myself, even after Korea, about trying to make an honest living. I'd been a bad kid, always looking for an edge. It remained my single most solid attribute. Wiseguys just don't happen. They're made. After the war I'd set about making myself.

I'd moved to Yonkers, New York, but got run out of town after some trouble with the local bookmakers and shylocks. Since my wife, Bunny, and her people lived on Long Island, Glen Cove is where I bounced.

Hook and Zabie were associates—not made members—of the Colombo Mafia Family, paying rent to Buster Aloi, a Colombo capo. I was doing their "sheet writing" over the phone. That is, I took the bets.

"We had a good week, Hook," I told him. "We even beat Chubby."

Chubby, a Queens bookmaker who laid off some of his horse bets with us, was also a big bettor himself. When he called, he was

good for $10,000 to $15,000 a day. And he only bet hot horses. Chubby always knew when the fix was in. He killed us.

"We beat Chubby for forty-eight thousand and some-odd," I told Hook. "And we beat six runners and the eight strays that called in. Our only loss is to the old man, Vito. Vito wins three hundred and change."

Hook smiled and shook his head. "That Vito is a weekly bill, like rent. Thank God he don't bet that much!"

I was doing good, pulling in about $250 a week from the diner, another $300 writing the afternoon track sheet, and another $300 sheet writing the trotters at night.

Then I took a pinch. The cops busted down my door and arrested me for bookmaking and possession of gambling paraphernalia. Misdemeanors, a bullshit pinch. But they lifted a couple thousand out of my pocket, collections for Hook, and swiped another $400 out of my wife's purse that she was saving for Christmas. Hook and Zabie paid her back the next day.

I was now unemployed. For one week. After that I worked the phones from a friend of my wife's house. She was a German girl. Good-looking woman. Hook and Zabie paid her phone and rent, so she was happy.

"Joe, you have an emergency phone call."

The caddy master was careening his golf cart down the thirteenth fairway. I was a golf fanatic; good at it, too. I had an eight handicap. The caddy master breathlessly informed me that the hospital was on the phone. Bunny had delivered a baby boy. Joseph Iannuzzi III. It was November 26, 1967. I rushed to the hospital—six or seven hours later. After all, my partners and I had to celebrate in the clubhouse first.

My *compare*—my godfather, my rabbi, the guy who looked after me—at that time was Mike "Midge" Belvedere, a bookmaker in West Babylon, Long Island. Midge was also connected to the Colombo Crime Family. Midge and his wife, Ann, were my son's god-

parents. Midge was a good-looking guy, a bronze Sicilian with thick, wavy black hair and dark, dark eyes. Almost black. When he stared at you, you felt like knives were going through your head. Midge dressed well and played the gangster role to the hilt.

His wife, Ann, was beautiful. She looked like Elizabeth Taylor, but with a better body. But once she opened her mouth, *marrone,* if you weren't looking at her you'd think a truck driver had joined the conversation.

Once when we were all vacationing in Florida, coming out of a hotel after seeing Sergio Franchi perform, the television actress Joi Lansing pushed through the mob waiting for the valet to bring around their cars. Joi Lansing smiled at Midge and gave him the eye. Ann sidled up to her slowly and said, "If you don't take your fuckin' eyes off my husband, I'll smack you in the face with your own big tit, you fuckin' whore." Ann was beautiful.

So I was managing the Bonton diner in Babylon and doing the figuring for Midge when one day he asks me to take a ride with him to Queens to buy some shoes. But instead of going to Queens, Midge drove to Brooklyn, where he bought four pairs of alligator loafers. I think he spent $800 or $900. While we were heading back to the car, a guy stopped Midge, hugged him, kissed him, and the two began talking and laughing.

"Frankie," Midge said finally, "meet a very close friend of mine, Joe Diner." Everybody had to have a nickname, including Frankie, whom I recognized as "Frankie Five Hundred," one of the biggest bookmakers in New York.

"Hi, Joe," Frankie said, sticking out his hand. "Come and join me for dinner, the both of you. I got to meet with that cocksucker Smitty at the Cypress Gardens restaurant, and I hate that fuckin' bum. But he's my capo, and I have to pay the rent."

Midge tried to talk me into it, but I had to be at work myself that night at the diner, and I couldn't afford to lose the job. I offered to take a cab home to free up Midge to eat with Frankie Five Hundred, and at one point Midge even insisted on paying the fare, handing me thirty dollars. But at the last minute he changed his mind, explaining to Frankie he "had to give the Mrs. a break."

So we said our goodbyes, Midge dropped me off at work, and he went home. Business was slow after dinner, and I was listening to the Yankee game on the radio when a flash bulletin came on.

"Tonight at Cypress Gardens restaurant an unidentified gunman killed three people while they were eating dinner. Police say the weapon used was an automatic. Killed were James "Smitty" D'Angelo, an alleged captain in the Bonanno Crime Family, as well as his brother, Tom, a railroad conductor. Also killed was an alleged numbers kingpin only identified as Frankie Five Hundred. Tune in for more details after the game."

A few days later Midge and I went to Frankie's wake, where I met the Colombo capo Buster Aloi for the first time. Midge went on and on, telling Buster what a lucky charm I was, how if it hadn't been for me he'd probably have gotten whacked, too. Buster just looked at me and nodded.

The Promised Land

I left New York for Florida in 1968. There was a recession on, money was tight, real tight, and I'd been offered a job down south hanging drywall. Florida was wide open at the time, booming, and in the back of my mind I had the vague idea that it was time for me to go straight. But when I got down there I was flat broke, and the only job available was through an old friend who set me up with a drywall contractor who had "won" the bid to hang drywall on a nursing home construction site, and he hired me even though I didn't even have enough money in my pocket to join the union.

"Look, Joe," he told me, "when the union guy comes around, I'll let you know. Then you go hide. And if for some reason he finds you, I'll have my brother slip you his union card. Fuhgedaboudit, the guy's blind anyway."

The union delegate came around nearly every three days, and eventually the shop steward got wise to me. He was going to squeal, so I went and told my boss.

"Oh yeah, Joe? I'll fix that cocksucker. I'll call you when I need you." Then he laid everyone off, the shop steward last.

That was the law in Florida. If you wanted to replace a shop steward, he had to be the last man laid off. The next day my boss

made me the shop steward and hired every worker back—except the old shop steward. I didn't even have a union card, and I was the shop steward! Florida was my kind of place.

I took it upon myself to shake everyone down. I was what you might call a slugger. If a subcontractor wanted to drop off material, they had to pay me off. I shook them down even if they were union. And everybody paid. But mostly it was the non-union suppliers, who were always in a hurry to get unloaded without having to hire union guys and pay union wages to unload. I was pocketing between $600 and $800 a week, off the books, and I loved the job. When that nursing home was finally completed, I hated to see that job go.

In 1969 I bought a house in West Palm Beach. Four-bedroom ranch. Mostly cash. What little mortgage I took I put in my wife's name. Florida was my new home. I was happy being away from New York, and Bunny and the kids loved it. I was making a decent living in the drywall business, and before long I had lots of things going on the side. A little shylocking, a little bookmaking. Sometimes I was hired out just to provide a little muscle. I never minded smacking a guy.

Late in 1970, two years after I'd settled in, I got a call from Louie Esposito, a friend of Midge's as well as a Gambino Family associate. Louie tells me he's bringing eighteen people down from Babylon, New York, for New Year's Eve, and he wants me to find him hotel reservations in Fort Lauderdale.

"Louie, are you nuts?" I asked him. "It's the middle of the season. You know what they're going to want as a deposit?"

"Joey, give them whatever they want, and take off work. I'll pay you a hundred a day every day you take off."

I found all the rooms he needed in the Fort Lauderdale Holiday Inn, and when the gang arrived Louie announced that we were all going to the track the next day.

"What's open?" Louie asked.

"Gulfstream," I told him. "But, Louie, I can't go. I can't afford to miss work."

"Forget it, Joe. You're going. Here's two hundred. You bet with that."

Marrone, I thought to myself, this guy must be sitting pretty fuckin' good.

We went to the track the next day, and Louie is sending me to the window to bet for him. "Who do you like, Joe?" he asked.

I told him I liked this one horse with speed, and that he was a drop-down horse and should go all the way.

"Here's four hundred. Go bet him to win." He handed me eighty five-dollar bills. I looked at him and smiled.

At the window, I bet $410 on the horse to win. I wasn't going to lose all my money! The horse won and paid five to one—$12.60. Louie collected $2,520. I made sixty-three bucks. Hey, this was more than a day's pay back in the early 1970s.

"Did you bet him?" Louie wanted to know. "How much did you bet on him?"

I was too embarrassed to let him know I'd only laid out ten dollars. He must have read it on my face.

"Here, you fuckin' scaredy-cat, here's a hundred," he said, peeling off ten ten-dollar bills. "You picked the horse and you don't even bet it? I don't believe this."

Marrone, another hundred! Then he handed me a hundred five-dollar bills.

"Bet the three horse," he said. "And don't bet it all at the same window."

I go and bet, this time throwing on another hundred of my own. The three horse won and paid even money. I got back $200 and Louie took in $1,000. Louie had two more winners that day; I kept feeding those five-dollar bills into the window. When we got back to his hotel room he showed me an enormous suitcase filled with five- and ten-dollar bills. I found out later that the stash was his cut from the big Aqueduct racetrack armored car heist. The guy was a horse thief.

The year was 1972. Louie Esposito was on the lam from another big robbery attempt in New Jersey. He and another guy got a tip

that this house had over $2 million in cash stashed in the library room, and this tipster had always been solid with the information.

So Louie and the other guy dressed as Catholic priests and went to the house. They said their car broke down. After the maid let them in, they pulled guns and headed directly to the library, as they knew the layout from the tipster.

Sure enough, when they opened the library door there were stacks of cash lining the bookshelves. But apparently the lady of the house had heard what was going on, and she ran to the front door screaming, "Robbery! Robbery!" Before they could subdue her, the neighbors had heard her screams and called the police.

Louie said that within no more than two minutes there were squad cars all over the place. He and his partner fled into some woods behind the house. Louie hid in the rafters of a construction site all night. The cops caught his partner. Louie told me he was on the lam because he wasn't sure if his partner had given him up.

"But, Louie," I asked him, "what happened to all that money from the Aqueduct heist?"

"Are you kidding, Joey?" A queer look crossed his face. "My share of that was only eight hundred thousand. I went through that in a couple of months. Gee, though, I wish I could have paid off my house. Anyway, I have to find some work until I make another score. You got a job for me?"

I was at one of my construction sites.

"Yeah, sure, Louie, come and work for me and you just hide in one of the rooms on the job. I'm the foreman anyway, so you can stay there and it won't cost you anything. I'll even put you on the payroll."

"Good, Joe, thanks. But I got to get my own place soon. I want to bring my son down here with me. My wife's having trouble with him. He won't listen to anything she says. Fuckin' kid! I give him everything. I can't understand why he's like that."

"Yeah, Lou," I told him. "It's real odd that your kid is like that. I mean, considering that his father is a graduate of Penn State and all. Or is that the state pen?"

Louie looked at me like he didn't get it. That was all right. He was a good thief. He did a lot of payroll and safe jobs plus a couple

of real big stick-up robberies. I figured that sometime down the road he'd pay me back.

"Joe, answer the phone," Bunny said. "It's probably for you anyway."

"Hello?"

"Hello. Can I speak to Louie please?"

"Who?"

"Louie! Louie! Tell him it's Tommy A."

"I think you have the wrong number," I said. "There's no Louie here. What area code did you dial? This is Florida, you know."

"Yeah, I know," said the voice at the other end of the line. "My friend Louie gave me this number. He was supposed to be staying with a friend of his named Joe Diner. Is that you?"

"Nah. I don't know what you're talking about. You got the wrong number." I hung up.

Louie was in the backyard, so I went out and told him that I was pretty sure the law knew he was here. "Some guy named Tommy called up and asked for you. I told him he had the wrong number and hung up. You better be careful."

Louie started laughing. "Oh shit, Joey. I forgot to tell you. I told my friend T.A. about you, told him that I was coming to stay here for a while, until the heat died. I hope he calls back."

Just then the phone rang again, and I ran inside just in time to hear Bunny say, "Listen, mister, there is nobody here by the name of Louie Esposito."

I grabbed the phone from her. "Tommy, I'm sorry. Louie didn't tell me you were going to call. Here he is."

Louie talked for ten minutes and hung up. "Joe, T.A. says that what you did with the phone was very good. He commends both you and your lovely wife, and he wants to take you both to dinner. He'll be here tomorrow, and we're going out tomorrow night. You know a good restaurant?"

"Yeah, we can go to my cousin Ozzie's place, Alfredo's. In Boynton Beach."

"Oh, he'll like it there," Bunny chirped in. "The food is great."

In the meantime, Louie told me all about T.A., Tommy Agro, so I'd be prepared to not only talk to him but to keep an eye on his mannerisms. T.A., Louie said, had a tendency to flip out occasionally. Break into cold sweats. Start acting real buglike, like Jimmy Cagney in *White Heat*. He sounded like a real challenge to meet.

Louie also said that T.A. was "almost there"—that he was "proposed."

"He'll make it the next time the books open up," Louie told me.

I didn't know what he meant. Proposed? Books? What the fuck, I thought, is he getting married or something? But I went along with what Louie was saying, pretending to understand what the hell he was talking about.

"Wow, that's great. Really? The next time the books open, huh?"

I didn't have a clue.

Tommy A.

"Hi, Joey, how are you? Louie told me a lot of good things about you."

You'd never know by looking at Tommy Agro, alias T.A., alias Tom Ambrosio, that he was to become the single greatest influence on my life. He was a squat, florid little man, standing five feet three inches on the tip of his toes. On this tiny frame he balanced a set of incongruously large shoulders, with a belly to match. He had a headful of thick, wavy black hair that must have looked beautiful on the horse it came off of. And though he wore elevator shoes to bring him closer to the sky, he was still always the last one to know it was raining.

T.A., a few years older than me, was an immaculate dresser, smooth and sharp. As they say, he was "All Mafia," and his mouth and mannerisms let you know it. Though lacking in any formal education, Tommy was an extremely street-smart person. But if you didn't know him, he could fool you into thinking he was a college grad.

"Hi, Tom, this is my wife, Bunny. Louie told me how close you two are. Please excuse the way I talked to you on the phone, but I had to be careful. You know what I mean."

"Of course, Joey, like I told Louie—you did the right thing. Hello, Bunny. Louie tells me you're a very good cook."

Tommy was accompanied by a tall blond flight attendant, and she was a knockout. Young, dumb, and full of cum, I thought.

So after I had a few Scotches in me, I asked Tommy if he'd mind if I danced with his girl. The music had started, and Phil Tolatta, the manager/maitre d', was singing "Strangers in the Night."

He looked at me screwy for a moment, then he laughed and said, "No, Joey, go right ahead. Sandi, dance with Joey. But be careful, don't hurt him. Because Bunny looks like she'll kill you."

As we were dancing, Sandi told me that I was the first man who had ever asked her to dance in Tommy's company. "Aren't you afraid of him?" she asked. "Everyone else is."

The evening ended great, everyone had a wonderful time, and as we were all saying our goodbyes I invited Tommy and Sandi to be my guest the following night. Tommy quickly agreed.

"I can't make it tomorrow night," Louie said.

"That's okay, Louie," I told him. "I'm old enough to go alone."

I took Tom and Sandi to the Palm Beach Kennel Club for dinner. The club was at the dog track, and I loved gambling on the dogs. I was pretty good at it, too, and Tommy was impressed by the way I picked winners. So impressed, as a matter of fact, that he asked to go again.

After the races, we went back to Alfredo's for dinner, and Tommy and I started to get a little closer in our conversation.

"Joey," he said, "if you know of anyone who wants a loan, you know, they pay the juice every week, you let me know. But they have to be solid. You know what I mean? And you can earn off the money, too."

"How much interest—or juice, as you call it—do you charge?" I asked him.

"Joey, it's all according to how much they want and whatever we can get without having problems. You know what I mean?"

"Yeah, well, I think I might know someone. A guy asked me the other day if I knew a shylock, and I told him no, not here in Florida. But I could tell him about you, and you take it from there. I think he wants five thousand."

"All right, Joey. Listen, you know what you do? If he mentions it to you again, tell him you know someone, but don't tell him who it is. Tell him it's five points a week. That's two fifty juice a week. But don't go to him and tell him you know somebody. Wait till he asks you again. Believe me, Joey, he will.

"Here's my home phone number," Tommy said, pulling a scrap of paper from his pocket. "Call me if he wants the loan. But you can call me anyway, to say hello, if you want."

I put Tommy's phone number in my wallet, but then took it out again and rewrote the number in code. I wanted to impress him. I wanted to be just like him. I wanted to be in the Mafia next to Tommy. I was ga-ga over the fact that I was doing something for him. Tommy Agro had just become my idol!

Bunny must have noticed that I was acting weird. She squeezed my hand, kissed me on the cheek, and whispered to me to be careful.

I ignored her. I was with Tommy A. I felt strong.

The next night we went to the dog track again, and we won all night. We won enough to pay for dinner and to throw big tips around and still have a couple hundred dollars in winnings left in our pockets.

At the end of the night Tommy gave me my new name. "Joe Diner" had become "Joe Dogs."

"When You Eat Alone, You Die Alone"

Two weeks later Tommy was back down in Florida. He'd flown in immediately after I'd called him and told him he'd been right. Lou Masiello, the guy who'd asked me if I knew a shylock, had indeed come back again.

"Lou, you pay Joey here two fifty a week juice," Tommy told Masiello at the meet I'd set up. "Try and be prompt with it, as I don't want no trouble."

"Oh, don't worry, Tommy, I wouldn't do anything like that," Masiello protested. "I've borrowed money before. I just got a little tight. I'll probably only need it for a couple of months. And besides, I wouldn't do anything to hurt Joe."

"Look, Lou," said Tommy, balling up his fists. "Let me make myself clear to you. All Joe did was introduce us. He's just doing me a favor by collecting this money for me. It's more convenient that way. I have other guys down here who would gladly come to your home and collect the interest weekly. Do I make myself clear?

"Joe is with me, Lou," T.A. continued. "Do you understand the terminology when I say 'with me'?"

Masiello seemed to indeed understand Tommy's terminology. Myself? I wasn't too sure on the specifics, though I caught the general drift.

As Tommy continued, a fine line of sweat appeared across his forehead. "Lou, it just dawns on me, what the fuck am I explaining these things to you for? You want the loan on these terms, you got it. If not, forget it, and I don't ever want to see you again. *Capisci?*"

"Yeah, Tommy, I understand," Masiello stammered. "I don't want you to be mad at me. I want to be your friend. Honest, Tom."

"Good, Lou, then we're friends. You see Joey every week, and we stay friends, okay? Now shake my hand and take the money and go. I have some business to talk over with Joe."

After Masiello left, I had one brief flash of nerves, wondering what I was getting into. Was this how I wanted to be? Was this the life I wanted to live? I was forty-one, at an age when other guys were settled in, just approaching the peak of their careers. Here I was joining the Mafia. Yes, I decided. Tommy had handled Masiello so professionally. He was so suave and sharp. He not only really told Lou how it was, he told Lou that I was with him! *With him*. I felt great, like King Kong.

"Joey, I have my wife flying down here tomorrow," Tommy said, interrupting my reverie. "I told her all about you and Bunny, and she wants to meet you. Tomorrow night we all go out, but tonight you and me talk. We'll have some drinks. Shoot some shit."

On the way to the bar we stopped at my house to tell Bunny about Tommy's wife, Marian, and our dinner date tomorrow.

"But tonight's boys' night out, honey," I added. "Don't worry, no women."

"There'd better not be," Bunny answered, but she was looking at Tommy. "By the way, Tommy, did you tell your wife about Sandi when you told her about Joe and I?"

Tommy looked at her and laughed. Then he said, "No, darling, and don't you tell her either."

He was no longer laughing.

. . .

I took Tommy to the Holiday Inn just down the block from my house, and we went into the lounge and had a few drinks.

"Joey, I want you to relax," T.A. told me. "I know you're trying to impress me, but don't knock yourself out. I'm impressed with you, and I'm impressed with your wife. I like the way you handle yourself. Now here is what I want you to do. Find yourself some more customers like that guy Lou. Expand yourself. Do things. And if you have any problems, call me. I'll help you. But on the other hand, if you do good, don't forget me. Because I have my own *compare*, and I can't forget him.

"In this life," Tommy continued, "when you eat alone, you die alone. Remember this, remember what I'm telling you. You think you knew people before? Forget about them. You belong to an organization now that is the biggest. So when I tell you to expand and do things, always be careful. Don't get hurt.

"If someone gives you a problem and you see you can't handle it, walk away. Never do anything foolish, because it doesn't pay to get pinched for something that can be handled differently. Joey, when you're with me, there is no one in this fuckin' world that can fuck with you. Not even the Pope! I swear on my daughter Kimmy."

I was almost swooning as Tommy lit my cigarette. Hook and Midge and even Louie Esposito, they were nothing compared to Tommy Agro. The guy had—how else can I put it?—class!

We met Marian the next day, and the four of us went to (where else?) the Kennel Club. We won again; I was on a roll. Bunny and Marian got along great, but then everyone got along with Bunny. She was a good lady, and I never went anywhere without her.

"That is one of your detriments," Tommy told me just before he flew back up north. "Joey, don't be bringing your wife along with you all the time. It don't look good."

Staking Out
the Gold Coast

Over the next couple of years I became Tommy Agro's top guy in Florida. The state was virgin turf back then, except for Miami, which had a legacy stretching back to Meyer Lansky and Joey Adonis; and the Gold Coast strip between North Miami and Palm Beach was exploding economically. Ripe for the plucking.

I was making a little book. Collecting for union no-show jobs. I had my fingers in some crooked horse races. And I had about eight good shylock victims in the streets. Even Lou Masiello, our first customer, had extended his loan to $12,000 and was paying $600 a week in juice.

People in the Palm Beach County area knew who I was. I was treated with great respect. I was also feared. I could be a son of a bitch, but only to those who didn't toe the line. It was part of the business. I didn't necessarily enjoy it, but if someone owed money and didn't pay, I knew how to break a leg. Because of all these factors, whenever I walked into a restaurant or a club, I was given the red-carpet treatment.

And I loved it.

If Tommy, who was staking out the Gold Coast for his faction of the Gambino Crime Family, had a problem with something

down south, he would call me and tell me to take care of it. Most of the time I could handle it myself. I didn't trust anyone else to do my work.

And along with frequent visits from T.A. himself, I began to meet different members of his crew. One of them was Bobby DeSimone, out of Hollywood, Florida. Bobby was what we called a "babe in the woods," a knockaround whore who will hang with any crew in any Family that will have him. He'd been with a couple of Families up in New York, and they had all chased him. Tommy told me he kept Bobby close to him because he felt "obligated." Obligated for what, he didn't say. I never turned my back on Bobby DeSimone.

Yet for all my tough-guy lifestyle, I was still perilously naive about the Mafia. For one thing, I didn't even know what Cosa Nostra Crime Family I was affiliated with. In 1973, during one of his visits, I finally popped the question to Tommy. I felt like a jerk, but I had to find out. I'd been pretending all along like I knew everything.

"T.A., what's our Family name?"

Bug-eyed, Tommy Agro laughed like hell at my question. Finally he told me that we were with the Gambinos, the largest Mafia Family in the United States, and that the head of the Family was Don Carlo Gambino. He went on to explain to me how the ranks in the Family operated.

There was Don Carlo, who, coincidentally, maintained a winter residence in West Palm. Directly below the Don was, naturally, the underboss. At the time, that was Aniello, or Neil, Dellacroce. Third in command was our *consigliere,* or counselor, Joe N. Gallo. Although in theory the *consigliere* had no official power of his own in the Family and derived his clout solely from the boss, in fact Gallo had several key Family duties to perform, including presiding over Family disputes and sit-downs between capos. He often had to decide who got whacked and who didn't.

The next rung down was occupied by captains, or capos, who each ran their own crew. In these crews were made guys, or buttons, or wiseguys, who had been formally inducted into the Mafia. These crews also included associates, who hoped to make their button when the bosses opened the books. If a captain had more

than one wiseguy in his crew, which was usually the case, he appointed one as his lieutenant. Of course, all of the buttons had their own crews, and some members of those crews even had their own crews. It was all kind of confusing at first.

But one thing was for certain. Getting a button was all these guys lived for. It was their badge of honor. You could only get "made" if you were of pure Italian extraction. But that didn't stop capos and soldiers from hiring on Jews, micks, even the occasional spade, as part of a crew.

Tommy, for instance, didn't have his button, and belonged to the crew headed by the longstanding Gambino capo Joe "Piney" Armone, who got his nickname back in the 1930s by shaking down the sidewalk Christmas tree sellers on New York's Lower East Side. But that didn't make me a member of Armone's crew. I owed fealty to Tommy Agro and Tommy Agro alone. What happened over his head had nothing directly to do with me. Or so I thought.

After explaining all this to me, Tommy told me I was to forget everything he just told me. Forget to ever mention it again, he meant.

"Here's how it works," Tommy said. "If you went out and made a score—dope, robbery, extortion, hijack, whatever—and you made a hundred thousand, what would you do? Would you tell me? Or would you keep it to yourself? C'mon, Joey, I want to know."

I hesitated slightly, thinking it over briefly before answering.

"Well, Tom, to be honest with you, if I did something without your knowledge, I would give you a percentage of what I took. Wait, wait, don't interrupt me. I want to explain to you why. Because if for some reason I ran into a problem or had some difficulty, I would have to turn to you for help."

As I was saying this, I reached into my jacket pocket, pulled out an envelope, and slid it across the table.

I continued: "As I feel, you are like my employer, or *compare*. And for that reason, just because I don't have a problem is no reason not to reward you with a little something."

Tommy reached out and opened the envelope. He counted out $10,000, put it in his jacket pocket, and ordered two more drinks.

"What did you do?" he asked.

"Does Macy's tell Gimbels?" I answered. "Remember last year you introduced me to our two friends, Little Dom Cataldo and Little Vic Orena? Well, they were down a few weeks ago, and asked me to help them with a problem. It was no big deal, a cinch really, but I don't want to go into detail. I just figured since you introduced me, you deserve a share."

The waitress delivered our drinks, and Tommy stroked the crack in her ass with one hand while handing her a hundred-dollar tip with the other. Then he gave me a soft, appreciative slap in the face.

"Little Dom told me he needed you for something, and he and Little Vic commended you to me," Tommy said. "But that's all they said. They didn't tell me you earned with them. Dominick is a good man, Joey. He's like me, only with another Family. And little Vic, he's like my *compare*, a capo, with the same Family. They're with the Colombos, Joey."

"Tommy, Tommy, I didn't know. I thought they were with us. Did I do wrong then by going with them?"

"No, Joey, it's all right. They came to me first anyway. Which is the right thing to do. But even if they didn't, you proved yourself by sharing your loaf of bread with me."

Tommy always made me feel good. I didn't understand why people called him the "Fuckin' Maniac" behind his back. He was always calm with me. Although I did wonder about those pills that he was always popping.

Little Dom's
Boot Hill

Peekskill, New York, 1973.

"Christ, Joe, I told you to get a thirty-eight. This fuckin' thing is too big. I'm not gonna kill a fuckin' bear, you know."

Little Dom Cataldo and I were scrunched down in the front seat of his car waiting for the carriers to come out of the loan office with the satchel. Dominick had a tip. There was supposed to be between $80,000 and $100,000 in this deal. Little Dom had flown me up from Florida to serve as his wheel man.

"Hey, Dom, cool out. All I could get was a Magnum. Anyways, you told me you just needed it to scare somebody, not to use it."

"Yeah, I know, Joe, but you never can tell."

Little Dom Cataldo, who was trying to make his button in the Colombo Family, stood five feet eight inches tall. He had a nice build and looked a bit like the actor John Garfield. To look at him and talk to him, you'd never believe that the guy had murdered over ten people. "I put him in Boot Hill" was one of Little Dom's favorite expressions. It was not brag, just fact.

In fact, Dominick did have a favorite burial ground. A certain hill along the Taconic State Parkway twenty miles or so north of New York City. He told me he wouldn't trust anyone. If there was

someone he had to bury, he would lock them in the trunk of his car and drive to Boot Hill personally, check into a motel, sleep until three or four in the morning, then go out and dig the hole.

"Not deep, Joe, you know, three to three and a half feet. Like that, you know? Then put some lime over the body, cover up, throw some grass seed around, and leave. It takes like an hour, not too long.

"But, Joey, there was this one fat motherfucker, he was a Lucchese guy, the fat pig," Dominick continued, mentioning another New York City–based Mafia Family. "I hated this cocksucker and I finally got his closest guy to drive over to this joint where he was going to meet with this broad. His own guy, Johnny was his name, conned him.

"Anyway, when they get to this place in the parking lot, I walked up and popped him right there in Johnny's car. Johnny says, 'What the fuck am I gonna do with this big fuck now?' So I was thinking. I told Johnny I needed some help with this fat bastard. I tell Johnny to help me throw him in my trunk and we'll get a shovel and pick, and I know a spot upstate that we could bury him.

"Because, Joe," Dom tells me, looking all kinds of sincere, "it's not right that I leave the problem with Johnny. I mean, after all, he got the cocksucker there for me to whack, so it's only right that I help him get rid of the body, because what can he say to his *Famiglia?*

"So we drive to Boot Hill, and it's late when we get there. I show him where to dig, and tell him to dig it deep, 'cause the lime smells. He don't know what I'm talking about, so I tell him I'll be back in a couple of hours, to dig it five or six feet deep.

"I drive down to the motel where I usually stay and had a nap. I told the clerk to give me a call in two hours. When I got back there, it was like four-thirty in the morning, and Johnny must have dug over six feet.

"I drove the car as close as I could to the hole, then John and I carried the fat fuck up and threw him in.

" 'Oh shit, Johnny,' I says. 'I forgot to take his watch off, his ring, and his dough. No sense in burying them.' So Johnny says he would go and get them. He jumps in the hole and I shot him, too.

Put the lime in and then the dirt and then the seed. But I had a lot of dirt to spread around, because I had a two-story job there.

"Ha-ha, that's funny, Joey. A two-story job."

Little Dominick Cataldo cracked himself up. Then we saw the carriers leave the building.

"Here they come, Joe. Two of them. You know what to do. Go ahead."

It was cold out. I wore a black leather jacket and a pair of leather police gloves that were lined with lead. I staggered up to the car the carriers were entering, laid on the hood, and made retching sounds like I was going to puke. They stopped, reached for me, and one of them said, "Hey, you fuckin' drunk, get the hell off my car."

Little Dom was covering me. I punched the guy so hard I heard his jaw crack. Dominick shoved the magnum in the other guy's mouth and he passed out. Dom grabbed the satchel and we were out of there. It took a total of thirty seconds.

Dominick was driving, and I wanted to count the money. "No, Joey. Not here. Wait till we stop somewhere."

We drove to Bear Mountain, got a room in a motel, and counted out $143,000. He told me there wouldn't be any investigation over this because it was drug money. It was a wiseguy's money, and he wouldn't do anything, because his captain wasn't in on it. He was fucking his capo, so he would keep quiet.

Dom told me he was giving the tipster $23,000, so we split the remaining $120,000.

"Not bad, huh, Joe? For a few minutes' work?"

"No, pretty good. But hey, Dom, tell me something."

"Yeah, what, Joe?"

"When the guy went down in the hole to get the jewelry and you shot him, did you go down and get it yourself?"

"No, Joe. I don't make mistakes like that. I'm not a mercenary. What I do, I do for a reason. I'll never leave a body, Joe. The law is so intelligent today, they can find a clue easily. The way I do it, it's a lot of work, but I'm clean."

I had another question. "Hey, Dom, how come you asked me to help you here? You got a million guys you could use."

"Because, Joe, I don't want no one to know, not even my captain.

I already gave him enough money this year. Are you going to tell Tommy A. about this?"

"I see no reason to," I answered. "Fuhgedaboudit. I'll throw him a bone and tell him I did something down south."

"Yeah, Joe, good. The less people know, the better."

"It's dead," I said.

"He Knows I'll Hurt Him"

"Joey, I'm here at the apartment down south," Tommy A. said into the phone. "Don't tell anybody I'm here. Come and cook something for us, willya?"

It was late 1974. I'd been a member of T.A.'s crew for two years now. Tommy was on the lam for an extortion bit he'd done. A horse bettor had owed him a lot of money, and Tommy threatened him. Now they were looking for him. They wanted him to talk to the grand jury. It was amazing how these guys got their information about indictments about to be handed up. Tommy was holing up in his Hollywood apartment, waiting for the heat to blow by.

"Bunny, honey, I'm going out and I don't know when I'll be back." I tried to make it to the door before the same old argument started. I didn't make it.

"Joe, where you going now?" she said. "We used to be so happy when we were broke. But ever since you got involved with Tommy, I don't see you anymore. We used to go everywhere together and do everything together. But the last couple of years it's Tommy this and Tommy that. What's wrong with you?"

"Hey, look, I don't want no shit." I was tired of this fight. "I bought you this house. We have an expensive piece of property.

You have your own car, jewelry, money in the bank. What the fuck more do you want from me?

"Oh yeah," I added. "Don't forget the boat!"

Bunny was crying now. "I dread the day Louie Esposito showed up here. We used to be so happy. I hate all those bastards for ruining our lives."

"Okay, honey, listen, I'm sorry," I said. "I'll be back as soon as possible. I just can't tell you where I'm going."

"Okay, Joey. But call me. Please?"

I hated to see Bunny cry. She was always there at my side when I needed her. I'm no good, I'm thinking. I fuck around on her. I was never like this before. She's better off without me. But I do love her.

An hour later I'd forgotten all about the fight.

"Hi, Tom. What's new? Hi, Buzz, Louie, Bobby. How you all doing?"

"C'mon, cook something, you fuckin' suitcase," Tommy yelled. Terms of endearment.

"Okay, but I play every other hand of pinochle, or you fuckin' guys starve."

Every time Tommy came down we would meet at his apartment and play pinochle. I was the worst player. But after all, these guys had all been in prison, so that's all they did every day, play cards. Sitting around the table with Tommy were Louie Esposito, Bobby DeSimone and a guy named Buzzy who I had met on a couple of occasions. He never said his last name. I didn't ask.

DeSimone, the "babe in the woods" to whom Tommy felt "obligated," had done two stretches in the state pen. He was tall, thin, and had a mouth like a motor. "Skinny Bobby," they called him, and his pedigree was bad. Both his brothers were nuts, and aspiring members of the mob. Bobby was a wannabe. His brothers were oughtabes. Buzzy was also a tall guy, and Italian, despite the nickname. He was one good-looking fella. He didn't belong with this motley crew. Buzzy was a drug dealer.

"Here, Tom, this is for you." I handed him an envelope containing $5,000.

He opened it and asked, "What's this from?"

I didn't want to broadcast my business in front of the crew. I told Tommy I'd fill him in later.

DeSimone said, "Well, Joey, if you didn't want to tell Tommy in front of us, why did you give him the money now? Are you trying to make us look bad?"

Tommy wheeled in his chair. "Bobby, go wash your fuckin' mouth out with soap. At least Joey contributes. What do you ever do, you skinny fuck?"

"I was only kidding, T.A.," Bobby answered in that high-pitched whiny voice of his. "I didn't mean no harm."

"Well I wasn't kidding," Tommy screamed. "Keep your fuckin' big mouth closed tight. Buzzy, it's your bid."

"I open," Buzzy said, adding, "and, hey, Tom, that kid Bobby Anthony wants to talk to you about that . . . you know."

It was amazing. We were all together. We were all one crew. And we're all talking in code, like one of us is a cop. That's how we always talked.

"Yeah, okay, Buzz," Tommy said. "Do you know this guy?"

"Yeah," said Buzzy, "he's okay. He just got out. Did a ten-year bit for whacking that cop. Used to work in advertising. He's the one that made up that slogan for Virginia Slims, 'You've Come a Long Way, Baby,' or something like that. He got a million bucks for it."

"Yeah, that's nice," Tommy said. "What's he want with me?"

"I don't know. He's with the Harlem group, you know, Charlie and Jerry."

"Yeah, I know 'em. Tell them to come here next Monday. I hear they're staying in the Diplomat, spending all kinds of money."

"Look, Bobby," Tommy A. was saying to Bobby Amelia, alias Bobby Anthony, a small-time drug dealer with a Harlem crew. "You asked for this meet. You asked for this money. What's my end gonna be as an investor? I want to know."

Bobby Anthony shot a quick glance at his partner. Bobby had introduced him only as Rabbit. "Well, Tom, if you want to invest, then you guys share in the risk. If there's a bust and we lose the

dope, then you guys lose your money. But if you want to shylock us the money, then we're responsible. It's as simple as that. But if you invest, I can guarantee you at least ten times your money."

Tommy was cautious. "What, are you nuts? How do I know what you're doing? You guys can say you got ripped off and what the fuck can I do about it? Then we have trouble. I pass. Fuhgedaboudit."

"Well, Tom, here's what we can do." It was the Rabbit speaking. "You be a silent investor, and I'll guarantee personally that you get back a hundred fifty thousand profit in no more than two months' time. If not, we'll pay you your money back, plus five thousand, in two months."

"So you're gonna guarantee the money, huh?" Tommy answered. "And who the fuck are you? You're only sitting here because you're Bobby's partner, and I'm showing him the courtesy to let you in here. So don't go talking like an asshole."

I'm thinking to myself that Bobby Anthony was trying to manipulate Tommy. But I didn't know for sure, so I kept my mouth shut. I liked Bobby. He was a small, thin guy. Nice-looking. And a hell of a lot of fun. I think T.A. was a little jealous of Bobby Anthony.

Finally I broke the tension. "Look, Bobby, let us think it over for a while, and we'll let you know by Thursday. Three days from now. But for an answer right now, fuhgedaboudit. I would have to pass also."

I could tell Tommy admired the way I was talking. By now I felt secure enough to talk like that to these guys. I'd learned a lot. Bobby agreed to meet with us again Thursday, but Rabbit cut in and said he couldn't make it, he had to be in New York.

"Oh gee, what a shame," Tommy said. "Then maybe we should cancel."

Bobby Anthony grinned. He knew what Tommy was doing. He knew his partner was a mope. On the way out Bobby pulled me aside and told me to call him. After they left, Tommy asked us what we thought about the deal.

I answered first. "To be honest, Tom, at first I thought it sounded like a rip-off. But there's a lot of risk in dope. You have to take your chances by trusting people, or else show your face up front.

But I know you wouldn't want to get involved with that, would you?"

"Fuck no," Tommy said. "What, are you crazy? My *compare* told me to make money but don't show my face. Orders from the tall guy, you know who I mean. Not the top guy. You know, the under."

Here we go again with the crazy double-talk. Tommy was referring to his captain, Piney Armone, who took *his* orders from Neil Dellacroce, Carlo Gambino's underboss. Dellacroce was currently locked in a power struggle with Gambino's cousin Paul Castellano, alias "Big Paulie," to succeed the aging Don Carlo.

"Yeah," I said. "I know who you mean."

"Well, he's into this shit big-time, Joey. But not Carlo. The boss is very sick anyway. I don't know who will be the top guy when he goes. My *compare* tells me that he heard rumors that maybe Paulie will. I hope so, because I don't get along too well with Neil. He just has some kind of hard-on for me, so my *compare* told me to stay away from him."

"So what do we do with Bobby and his intelligent partner the Rabbit?" I wanted to know.

"Joey, we'll talk about it later. Let's go pick up the girls."

My date's name was Anna. Tommy's was Tracy. Two young broads. Anna was pretty, about five nine, slim, nice ass and legs, no tits, and dark hair. I was tired of blondes. Tracy was a tiny blonde with big tits and a big ass. Tommy loved them small. We went to the dog track, Biscayne in Miami, and we won again. We let the girls keep the winnings, about $300 apiece.

"See, Joey," Tommy told me at one point during the night. "These girls are nice. I don't go with hookers. I don't pay to get laid."

I thought about the expensive dinner and the $600 from the track, and I told Tommy to stay out of the sun tomorrow. "Your head is getting baked."

The next day we decided to go in on the deal with Bobby Anthony. Tommy didn't see it as taking much of a chance. "I don't think he'll fuck with me," he said. "He knows I'll hurt him."

We arranged a meet at my house in West Palm, but Tommy

didn't want Bobby Anthony coming into the house. He didn't like the fact that I was so friendly with people from all the Families. He wanted me for himself.

"Joey, they just want to make you a rent job," he'd tell me, meaning that anybody could use me for anything anytime they pleased. "You're part of my crew."

Frankly, I think he was a paranoid schizo, not to mention becoming a pain in the ass. I liked a lot of people. I liked Bobby Anthony. Tommy always wanted to know what I was doing and who I was doing it with. Oh, he used to try to couch it, saying things like he had to know everything I was doing because if I got whacked he'd have to retaliate. But I knew he just wanted his piece of the pie.

Bobby Anthony showed up at my house on time, and Tommy made him conduct business on the front stoop. Bobby shot me a glance like Tommy was nuts, but shook it off and went into his spiel.

"Here it is, Tommy. I talked it over with my partner," Bobby began. "I know you don't like Rabbit, but I do, and personal feelings don't come into this. I'm not too crazy about you myself, but business is business. You give us fifteen thousand, and we give you back ten times that in no longer than two months. But if something happens bad with the deal, we pay you back the fifteen thousand plus five thousand juice. That's it. Take it or leave it."

I admired the way Bobby Anthony spoke to Tommy. Not disrespectful, but straight. He showed Tommy that he wasn't afraid of him.

"Give him the money, Joey," Tommy said. "Count it in the car and get outta here."

Bunny cooked dinner that night, and at the table Tommy made contingency plans.

"Joey, if Bobby fucks up, I'll take care of it. I don't want you getting involved. I got to go in for a year on that bookmaking bit, and I need you out here to be my eyes and ears. So you don't do nothing, understand? He fucks up, I'll reach out and take care of it. Gee, Bunny, this is good. Is it what the Jews eat?'"

"No, Tommy," Bunny said. "Jewish people don't eat pork."

"You See Tommy Coming, You Kill Him. Okay?

Tommy Agro was the kind of guy even his best friends didn't want to cross. I found out firsthand just what kind of crossed wires this guy had about a week after we did the deal with Bobby Anthony. Bunny and I went to the Diplomat Hotel in Hollywood, Florida. A friend named Jiggs Forlano had called saying he wanted to see me about some business we were doing, so we decided to make an evening of it with our wives. I had called ahead to the Tack Room, and Tony, the maitre d', had, as usual, saved me the front center table.

Nick "Jiggs" Forlano was a retired capo from the Colombo Fam-

ily, or as retired as a capo can get. He was very low key, very quiet, very deadly. He'd been notorious in his day, and the word on the street was that he'd refused the leadership of the Colombo Family when Joe Colombo got shot back in '71, and instead grubstaked a claim in South Florida. I got along great with him. Jiggs and his lovely wife, Sophie, were waiting for us in the lobby of the Dip when we arrived.

We were sitting in the Tack Room when Bobby Anthony walked in, and I invited him to join us for a drink. When I introduced him to Jiggs and Sophie, Bobby embarrassed me, telling Jiggs how he'd heard what a real killer he'd once been. I felt uneasy but managed a laugh. Jiggs just stared at him, chewing on an unlit cigar.

"Yo, wait a minute, Cap," Bobby said nervously. "I was only kidding. I got a big mouth."

Jiggs nodded in agreement, then broke into a smile. "Okay then, sit down and be quiet before I tell your boss Gerry to spank you." He was referring to Bobby's boss in Harlem.

The next to arrive was Bobby DeSimone with his wife, Betty. I asked him where Tommy was.

"He'll be right here, Joey," DeSimone said. "But he doesn't know you're out tonight. He'll be surprised to see you."

"I tried to call him," I told DeSimone, "but his line was always busy."

"That's no excuse, Joey," said the motormouth. "You know Tommy has two phones." This asshole hated my guts because Tommy and I got along so well.

Moments later Tommy walked in with Louie Esposito's girl, Lily. Louie had flown back to New York on business, and although Lily was the biggest blowjob in Queens, Tommy had decided to escort her. Now that I think of it, that's probably *why* Tommy had decided to escort her.

"Tom, sit down," Jiggs said. The table was packed, but we squeezed in two more.

Tommy looked us over, saw Bobby Anthony and all the others, shook hands with Jiggs, gave Sophie a kiss, and ignored me.

He sat right across from me, and I said, "Hey, buddy, what's wrong? Don't you feel good?"

"Yeah, I feel fine," he answered without looking at me. He had something on his mind, and I didn't like the way he was acting. He put a cigarette in his mouth, I struck a match to light it, and he slapped my hand away and lit it himself.

Ten minutes went by and Tommy put another cigarette in his mouth. I struck another match. He smacked my hand down, harder this time, and said, "I'll light my own cigarettes. Go light your friend's there." He pointed to Bobby Anthony.

Minchia, I thought. My cock! I was pissed off, and a little concerned.

I excused myself from the table, walked into the Celebrity Room, and asked Miguel, one of the Cuban waiters, for a boning knife. I told him I had to cut a piece of leather off my wife's shoe. I wanted to be prepared in case Tommy started anything. He was notorious for always carrying a pair of sharp scissors.

I returned to the table, the knife in my left waistband with my jacket covering it. The floor show was over, and Jiggs and Sophie were leaving. Jiggs and I hadn't had a chance to talk, so we made plans to meet at the track the following day. As I was saying goodbye, Tommy made his way over to the bar. Ten minutes later I heard him calling me over.

"Yeah, Tom, what's up?"

He started kicking me in the shins, screaming, "I'm gonna teach you a fuckin' lesson!"

I couldn't believe what was happening. I never took any bullshit from anyone in my life. Here I show this guy a world of respect, and he's doing this to me in a public place? I reached back and gave him a karate chop in the forehead with the heel of my hand. He went flying on his ass, and his rug slipped halfway off his head.

He got up to charge, reaching into his back pocket, and I grabbed the handle of my knife with my right hand. I lunged my right arm back and forward, like throwing a softball, and as the boning knife was closing in on his groin I was suddenly grabbed by an undercover cop I knew from the area.

"Take it easy, Joe," the cop said to me, and by this time there were people holding Tommy back, too.

Tom left the Diplomat with Lily, but the maitre d' and manager suggested I wait awhile before I headed out. Bobby Anthony had stayed in my corner. But Bobby DeSimone and his wife trailed out behind T.A., DeSimone shooting me a dirty look on his way toward the door. Bobby Anthony caught the look and asked if DeSimone had something he wanted to settle outside. The motormouth declined and scurried through the door.

Bunny was scared as hell, so ten minutes later the maitre d' led us out a secret door through the kitchen. Bobby Anthony came with us and in the parking lot asked me if I had any weapons at home. "Yes," I answered, and on the drive home Bunny asked if I really thought Tommy would come after me at the house.

"I don't know, honey, but don't worry. I'll take care of it. I guess I should have listened to you a long time ago."

"I'm not going to say I told you so. But I told you so."

We both laughed nervously as I pulled into the driveway.

"Joe, honey, come to bed. It's three in the morning."

I was sitting by the front window with a thirty-thirty rifle, a carbine, and a forty-five pistol. I wasn't taking any chances. I was afraid Tommy A. would retaliate right away. Bruno, our 160-pound brindle-colored Great Dane, haunched next to me.

"You go to sleep, honey," I whispered to Bunny. "I'll be in in a little while. I'm a little worried."

"Joe, he won't hurt the children, will he? I'm so scared. Why don't we call the police?"

"The cops!" I exploded. "Are you crazy? What are they going to do, you fuckin' idiot. They know who I am. They know who I'm connected with. They'll come here and laugh at us. You think they care what happens to us? Besides, I don't call the law. That cocksucker comes near here, I'll kill him myself. Now go to bed. You're pissing me off."

I hated to talk to Bunny that way. But I was really worried and taking my anxiety out on her. I couldn't believe it had come to this between Tommy and me. Twenty-four hours earlier there hadn't been anything I wouldn't do for the man.

"Joey, it's six-thirty. Come to bed and don't yell at me," Bunny called from the bedroom.

I smiled. She was a good person. She deserved better than me. She wasn't materialistic. All she wanted was for me to love her and be faithful to her. I had been, too. Until I became a Mafia tough guy.

"Okay, honey," I told her. "I'll come in on one condition: You see Tommy coming, you kill him. Okay?"

"How about I just wake you up?"

I slept with the forty-five next to my pillow. I dozed off into a coma and dreamed about being bayonetted in Korea. At five that afternoon Bunny shook me awake. Jiggs was on the phone and needed to talk to me.

"Joey, I thought you were supposed to meet me at the track today. What happened? You know I had to talk to you about that thing you asked me about."

Christ, I thought. Here was a capo doing me a favor, and I forgot all about it. I had swiped some diamonds, and I wanted to get rid of them. I didn't want to fence them through T.A., because he'd have glommed them. That's why I'd gone to Jiggs.

"Jiggs, I'm sorry. I just woke up. Did you hear what happened at the Dip last night after you left?"

He hadn't. I explained.

"Joe, did you have to pull that knife on him?" Jiggs asked. "That makes things difficult."

"Jiggs, I did what I had to do. He was going for his pair of scissors. I sat up all night with a bunch of guns waiting for him to come over."

Jiggs laughed at that. "He's not that stupid, Joe. Anyway, I'm going to see him. You stay home, don't go anywhere, and wait for my call."

Three hours later Jiggs called back.

"You know what happened, Joey? When Tommy saw you with that doper Bobby Anthony, he thought you were doing something behind his back. I told him he should put his arm around you and see that no one bothers you because of the money you earn for him. Now here's what I want you to do. Tomorrow morning at eleven

o'clock you be at Tommy's apartment. I'll be there. I want the two of you to talk out your differences and settle this dispute. But be there at eleven, because I got to get to the track."

"Jiggs," I said slowly, "nothing is going to happen, is it? I'm going to come dressed, you know what I mean?"

I was telling Jiggs I'd arrive carrying a gun.

"Joey, I told you, I'm going to be there. If you bring anything into my presence I'll make you eat the damn thing. *Capisci?* Don't be late."

"Always Watch Your Back"

I left West Palm Beach at nine-thirty the next morning. The drive to Hollywood took an hour and fifteen minutes. I parked my car and sat in the underground lot for eight minutes. At three minutes to eleven I knocked on the door of Tommy's eleventh-floor apartment.

I didn't come "dressed."

Tommy opened the door, and as I entered he was walking away from me. No hellos. No embracing. No nothing. I followed him into the dining room, where Jiggs was already sitting. I was scared.

"I want you two to shake hands and discuss whatever problems you have," Jiggs began. "I don't want to hear no arguing, no threats, no involvement physically. If I hear or see any of these things, you will have to deal with me, and I don't think you want that. Now I'll be out on the balcony, so get started. And make it as quick as possible, because I got to get to the track. Talk nice, boys."

I spoke first.

"Tom, I don't know why this happened and I'd love to forget about it and resume our relationship the way it was. You know I care for you like a brother. I've proven what I would do for you whenever you've asked."

"Joey, I don't know what you're doing with that Bobby Anthony, and I don't care. I'm just going to tell you one more time. Be careful of him. He's bad people. Him and his fuckin' idiot partner Rabbit."

"But Tom, I—"

"Just a minute, Joey. I'm not finished. When I finish, I'll listen to you. But right now I have the floor. You know that seventy-five thousand you've got of mine, the money you say is shylocked out on the streets? I want it all back in. You have one month to get it in. And not only that, I want the names of all the customers you got, and where they live."

So this, I thought, is what the motherfucker wants. My mind worked overtime. He was talking like he was doing me a favor by lending me $75,000 at 1½ percent per week. I was handing over more than $1,100 in juice every week. He wanted it in one month. Well, fuck him. I'd get it back to him tomorrow. I had money this asshole had no idea about.

"With all due respect, Tom," I answered, "I'll do the best I can. But as far as my customers go, I won't give you their names or their addresses. They're mine, not yours. Now, I pay you eleven and change every week, so if you're willing to give that up, I'll have your seventy-five grand by tomorrow. You know the good standing I have with the Colombos—there's one of them on the balcony right now—well, I can always go to work for them.

"And as far as the bookmaking out at Gulfstream, that was my idea. You want that, too? Who's gonna run it? That skinny fuck DeSimone you got hanging around you? He doesn't have the brains of a flea.

"And those two paychecks I send once a week from the no-show union jobs out at Century Village? That's about six bills clear every week. Do I find a new *compare* to collect for the absent Mr. Russo and Mr. Demarco, Tom?

"Would you like me to go on?"

Tommy stared at me for a minute and then sprang for me. He hugged me and kissed me on both cheeks. "Joey, I just wanted to see what kind of man you were. And you are a man."

We both laughed and hugged and Jiggs walked in smiling. "All

right, that's enough," he said finally. "You look like a couple of *finocchios*." Jiggs hated fags.

We made our goodbyes, and on the way down in the elevator Jiggs turned to me and said, "I'm glad you two are friends again, Joe, but listen to me good. Be careful. Always watch your back. I won't say any more, and don't ask me no questions."

Then he changed the subject.

"As far as those stones go, yeah, they're good, and no, I did not mention them to your *compare* upstairs. But the best I can do is five thousand a stone. They're all about a carat apiece and worth three times that amount. But you know how it is. Everyone down the line has to earn a little money."

"Okay, get rid of them," I said, handing Jiggs a bag containing twenty-six diamonds. He promised to have the money for me in a week. We set a date to meet at the track.

Gulfstream had just closed for the 1974 meet, and they were racing at Calder Race Course in Miami. That's where I met Jiggs a week later. He handed me $130,000 cash for the diamonds. I thanked him and gave him $20,000 for his trouble. He tried to give it back, saying he'd merely done me a favor, but I told him if he didn't take it I'd leave it for the waitress.

"You bastard," Jiggs said as he picked up the dough.

Ruby Stein was Jiggs's main tenant. By tenant I mean someone who pays rent. It was said that in any given week Ruby Stein had $2 million on the streets, mostly shylock loans to wiseguys and big businessmen. If that was true, and I had no reason to doubt it, it meant Ruby was pulling in $20,000 a week in juice alone. They said Jiggs took 25 percent of that, or $5,000 a week, which provided him with a nice little nest egg of a quarter million a year. And Jiggs needed every bit of it. He was a degenerate gambler.

"Hey, Joey, I've been watching this horse and he's going off four to one," Jiggs said. "I'm going to bet a G on him."

"Do that at the window, Jiggs, and he'll go off nine to five. Better to give it to Abbie Roth over there."

Abbie Roth had been the bookmaker at Calder for as long as

anyone could remember. He was the reason our crew didn't have our own bookmaker at Calder. Why start a beef?

"I don't want to meet nobody," Jiggs said softly. "Here, you take it to the Jew. As long as you say he's all right, that's good enough for me."

We both bet $1,000, and the horse went off at seven to two. He went wire to wire and paid $9.20. We won $3,060 apiece. We spent the rest of the day bullshitting about Families. Not families. When Jiggs found out I was close to some of the Colombos like Little Dom Cataldo and had even done some business with Little Vic Orena, he couldn't understand why I was still with Tommy A. and the Gambinos. I just shrugged.

At the end of the day Jiggs had won $5,800 and I'd pocketed $2,000. As we were leaving, he warned me one more time to watch my back.

"Uncle Joe, You're Crazy"

The mention of the no-show union job during my beef with Tommy reminded me that I had to start spending more time on the job site. I'd opened a drywall construction company in January of '74, my legit business on the side, and to this day I think I might have been a success as a "citizen" if I wasn't always in love with the easy buck. As it was, I left most of the construction duties in the hands of my brother Frank, who was also my foreman.

So the day after Jiggs and I cleaned up at the track I decided to run over to Century Village, where my outfit had won a bid to hang the drywall. I got to the construction trailer around one-thirty that afternoon and asked my niece Marsha, who I'd brought down from New York to be my secretary and bookkeeper, what was going on.

"Uncle Joe, most of the men were here at lunchtime," she reported. "They said they wanted their money. They say they want to quit. They say they won't work here as long as Uncle Frank is their foreman, or supervisor, or whatever it is he does."

Fifteen minutes later there were fifty-two construction workers outside the trailer complaining that my little brother—who carried 220 well-muscled pounds on a six-foot, two-inch frame—was shooting a pistol at them while they worked.

If there was one thing I wouldn't tolerate, it was insubordination from supervisors. So I confronted Frank right in front of the fifty-two men.

"Did you fire a gun at these guys, telling them you were going to shoot them if they didn't get up to work on that building's fourth floor?"

"Hey, Bro," Frank answered. "You think I would do anything like that. You know me better than that. They just don't like me because I'm Italian."

"Okay, end of story," I announced. "Whoever wants to quit, get the fuck out of here and pick up your pay Friday. Now either go to work or hit the fuckin' road. You got three minutes to decide what to do."

They all went back to work. They all made good money with me, and their checks never bounced. They also knew I could have replaced every one of them in less than three days. My payroll was between $50,000 and $60,000 a week. But the outfit I had the contract with sent their money in like clockwork.

Back inside the trailer, I turned to Frank and asked him what kind of gun he had used. "You fire a thirty-eight?"

"Nah," Frank said. "I used this little twenty-two pistol. No big deal."

"Oh, in that case, that's different." I smiled. "Let's go have a late lunch."

Marsha was aghast. "Uncle Joe, you're crazy. And Uncle Frank, I believed you! The both of you, you're terrible."

Frank and I just laughed and shook our heads.

Muscle

"Grrr. Grrr. That fuckin' girl." That was a soliloquy for Gino.

Gino was a big-built lob from Boston. I kept him around the construction site in case I needed some muscle. He had just done ten years inside, and he was good to have at your back. Gino had a lot of balls and would do anything I asked.

"What's wrong, Gino? What are you grumbling about?"

"That girl at the restaurant across the street, she don't want me to fix your coffee anymore. I told her you don't like it the way she fixes it, that she puts too much milk in it and you start yelling. But she says she don't want me touching the coffeepot no more.

"She also said that the manager don't want us in there no more. That we should go someplace else to eat lunch."

The "restaurant" across the street was the Deerfield Beach Country Club. It was built on a beautiful golf course, and catered to a real la-de-da lunch crowd. But it was convenient, right across from the job site, and I'd often take a bunch of supervisors to lunch in the club's dining room. In fact, I left such big tips that the girls were always scrambling to wait on our table. I thought we were liked over there. But one of Century Village's foremen was a good-looking black man named Johnny Coleman. I had a feeling this beef had something to do with Johnny Coleman.

"Gino," I said, "you go back over there and get me my coffee.

And if the girl don't fix it right, you take it and show it to the manager."

He was back in five minutes with the container. I lifted the lid. It was almost milk white.

"Gino, did you fix this coffee or did the waitress do this?"

"I didn't touch it, Joe. In fact, the manager told me to wait outside while she fixed the coffee."

"I don't fuckin' believe this. I'm going over there right now."

"Let me come with you," Gino said. I told him no in no uncertain terms.

When I walked through the door of the Deerfield Beach Country Club, the manager was waiting as if he expected me.

"Excuse me, sir," I said to the motherfucker. "I think we have a communications problem here. I've been sending one of my employees here every morning for—"

He interrupted me. "There's no communications problem. I feel that your presence is not desired here, and I will do anything to discourage your motley crew from coming here. As you can see, we cater to a different class of clientele."

I looked at this mook, staring at his jugular vein, wanting to rip it out. But I remembered T.A.'s advice. I stayed cool.

"Well, sir, I'm sorry to hear that," I told the cocksucker. I turned and wheeled out. When I reached the trailer I told Gino to find me Johnny Coleman. Right away.

Within minutes Johnny Coleman was standing at my desk. "Yeah, Joe baby, what's up?"

"John, how many niggers you got working here?" I asked him.

"Joe, man, don't call my men niggers. You know I don't go around calling you wops and all that shit."

"Sorry, John, my mistake," I said. "I just wanted to see if you wanted to make a hundred bucks for yourself and wanted to treat all your, um, blacks to lunch today and tomorrow."

I told him what had happened at the country club. And I explained my scheme. Then I sent Marsha to the bank with a $400 check, and she returned with eighty five-dollar bills. By 11:35 A.M. there were about fifty black guys standing in front of my trailer.

"Listen up, guys," I announced. "I'm going to give you five bucks each, and I want you all to take it across the street to that country club and order lunch. I want you all to go there and sit four to a table and act like gentlemen. But I don't want you to wash up here before you go. Use their washroom. Order your food, leave a tip, but don't take any shit. If anyone tries to throw you out, we'll call the NAACP and close them up. Remember, don't start no trouble. And be back here tomorrow at the same time. Lunch is on me again. But don't rat me out."

You had to see these guys! Two had holes in their pants and their cheeks were hanging out. Most had ripped T-shirts. They were a filthy mess of Zulu construction workers.

I returned from my lunch in town at two-thirty, and Johnny Coleman was waiting for me by the trailer.

"Joe, you should have been there. When we walked in, there was about a dozen regulars in there eating lunch. They got the fuck out of there in about fifteen seconds. Then we all sat down and ordered the same soup, but they ran out. Then we all ordered club sandwiches and the cook quit and ran out. Then, after we ordered, we went to the washroom—ten at a time—and we left that washroom so filthy the rats ran out.

"We acted nice and quiet and they still called the police. And, Joe, get this. Two of the cops that showed were black guys. I went up to them and asked what the problem was. I mean, we work across the street, and this was a public place and all, and with the manager standing right there I told the cops that we were planning on coming in for lunch every day. I asked the cops if they had any objections and they said, 'Fuck no.'

"Then the cops turned to the manager and told him they didn't appreciate the superficial call, and not to do it again."

The two of us rolled on the ground laughing.

I didn't have to wait long for results. Within an hour the big shots from Century Village were in my trailer. They had been called by the big shots in the country club. They knew I was behind the whole thing. They assured me that it was all a misunderstanding, and that my foremen and supervisors were of course welcome for

lunch anytime. As a matter of fact, they said, the manager of the dining room had been fired.

The next morning I summoned Johnny Coleman, threw him $200, and told him to take the black crew from the day before to lunch anywhere but the Deerfield Beach Country Club. Then I rounded up the rest of my foremen and supervisors and we returned to the club. Lunch was on the house. Even the cook had returned. There was only one difference: He had taken club sandwiches off the menu.

The Crew

In a way, being a member of a crew is like never leaving high school. The boys are all ganged up and strutting around like roosters, the girls are only food for fucking, and the jokes never get beyond the twelfth-grade level. I remember one Sunday during the spring of '74 when Tommy was still lamming it in his Hollywood apartment. I'd gone to his place to cook for him and the crew. We also had some business to discuss. After we ate.

"Joey," Tommy said, "the maitre d' at the Diplomat gave me these squid. You know what to do with them? My mother used to stuff them. You know how to make that?"

"Yeah, Tom, but you need a grinder to grind the heads up and stuff and we don't have one."

"Won't a blender do the same?" Buzzy asked.

"I don't know," I said. "I'll try it with a sharp knife. I can chop the heads and tentacles up pretty fine."

"Don't forget to remove the eyes, Joey," Bobby DeSimone said. "I think they're poisonous."

"They're not poisonous, you just don't eat them," I said.

"Tommy does," Buzzy said. "He eats eyes all the time. I just heard him tell this guy yesterday that if he didn't show up with the money he would eat the eyes out of his fuckin' head."

It was nice hanging around with the guys. Someone was always

joking. And when Tommy was in a good mood (which wasn't often), most of us made him the scapegoat of our jokes.

There were usually five of us, which meant that one guy would have to sit out of the pinochle game, then play the next game with one of the losers. No one wanted me for a partner. Hell, I couldn't remember ten cards, much less forty-eight, like they all did. They always screamed at me, but I didn't care. It was fun. And whoever lost the most had to do the dishes. I went out and bought a pair of rubber gloves. That should tell you something.

Midway through the meal, Tommy announced that the grand jury looking for him had "de-convened."

"My *compare* told me I have to come back in, so I'll be leaving this week," he said. "And just when I met this broad. What a living doll she is. I think she's about twenty-one. I gave her the number here, to the phone in the bedroom. She said she was gonna call today."

Tommy had two phone lines. The living room was for us guys to use. A business phone. The other, in the bedroom, was his "hot-line number." He only gave that number to his special girlfriends. We all had the number, but we never used it.

"Joey, you should see the ass on this baby doll," Tommy went on. "She is just beautiful. I think I'm in love."

I was sitting out of the after-dinner pinochle game and was wondering what kind of mischief I could get into. "Tommy, can I use your phone? I got to call Bunny."

"Go ahead, use the phone. And since when do you have to ask?"

I dialed the phone in the bedroom on the business phone, and it began to ring. Tommy thinks it's his broad. He got up from the table and walked nonchalantly into the bedroom. As soon as he reached the receiver, I hung up. He came out muttering, "Mother-fucker, they hung up. I bet you that was her."

"Don't worry, Tommy, she'll call back," Bobby said. "She probably thought you stepped out, because the phone rang five times before you picked it up."

"Joey, did you call your wife?" Tommy asked.

"The line was busy. I'll call back after we play this next game."

Tommy was my partner and he was aggravated because he hadn't reached the phone. He started nagging me about the card game. "What the fuck you coming in spades for, Joey? Don't you see me pointing to my ring? That means diamonds, you fuckin' idiot."

I'd seen him point but pretended I hadn't. I just wanted to get back on that phone. Whoever was sitting out of the game had the choice of picking his partner from one of the losers, and I was never picked. So I sat out. And dialed again.

Tommy got up a little quicker this time and started walking into the bedroom. "Ooh, ooh, I betcha that's my baby doll," he cooed.

I hung up on the fourth ring.

"Motherfucker, she hung up again."

"Hey, Tommy," I said helpfully, "don't take so fuckin' long to get to the phone."

"Joey, this is a big apartment. I got there as quick as I could. Son of a bitch."

"You know, Tommy, next time it rings, I'll run back there and get it for you," DeSimone said. "I can reach it by the second or third time."

"You don't answer that phone, Bobby. You'll scare her away with that faggot voice of yours. I'll run next time it rings."

I was laughing so hard I had to go into the kitchen. By now, Tommy's talking to himself. "Gee, I hope she calls back. I wanted to take her out tonight."

"Why don't you call her?" I asked him. "Don't you have her number?"

"I don't ever call broads, Joey. I give them my number. If they call, they call. But I never call them."

I lost another hand and Louie Esposito handed me my rubber gloves. "Here you go, Joey, your mittens. Make sure you get everything spotless."

Marrone, but I was tired of washing dishes. But I finished them, went back to the living room, and picked up the phone one more time. The phone in the bedroom began ringing.

Tommy jumped up and bolted for the bedroom. On the second

ring he tripped in the foyer. He crab-walked to the phone and got it on the fourth ring. I hung up.

"My fuckin' back," he moaned. "I think I hurt it bad. I think I'll knock the shit out of that broad when I see her."

"It's not her fault, Tommy," Bobby said. "I told you I should have answered the phone and this would never have happened."

"Shut the fuck up," Tommy said. "Joey, you going? I'll see you later. That squid was good. Is there any left?"

"Yeah," I answered. "In the fridge. That maitre d' gave you enough to feed an army."

When I got home I told Bunny what I'd done. We both laughed for an hour. But now, how was I going to let Tommy in on the joke without getting killed? The gag was no good unless he knew about it, and I knew he wouldn't think it was funny. I waited until about eight o'clock that night and called him.

"Hiya, Tip. How you feeling? Your girl call back?" Sometimes I called him Tip, short for Tommy.

"Nah, Joey, the bitch never called. She probably got tired of dialing. Anyway, the back's a little better. But I took some fall. All over a fuckin' broad. You coming to the Diplomat tonight?"

"Maybe, Tom, but listen, first I got to level with you. That girl never called you."

"What do you mean? How do you know? It could have been someone else. But what makes you say it wasn't her?"

"Because, Tom, it was me dialing the bedroom from the living room."

"Joey, you motherfucker," he screamed. "You made me almost break my fuckin' neck! You come down here right now. I'll break your fuckin' head! Get down here, Joey! That's an order!"

"Fuck you," I laughed. "There's no way I'm coming there now. You cool off first, and think about how funny you looked. You really fell head over heels for that girl."

"Joey, I'm gonna rip your fuckin' heart out," he said, but by now even Tommy was laughing a little. Then he hung up.

I told Bunny he'd get over it, and we'd all have a good laugh about it someday. Nevertheless, I stayed home that night.

My First Enemy: The *Consigliere*

Tommy called the next day, laughing. "I can't believe I fell for that shit. I should have known, all those calls to your wife. Anyway, the girl showed up at the Dip last night and I told her about your gag. She laughed like hell. She said all the guys she meets with me act like they're in a gangster movie. Are you coming in tonight? I want to talk to you. I'm leaving tomorrow."

I drove to the Diplomat that night to meet T.A., and he grilled me with all kinds of questions about how I met Jiggs. I told him a mutual friend, a big South Florida bookmaker named Freddie "Freddie Campo" Campagnuolo, another babe in the woods, had introduced us at a Sinatra show the previous New Year's Eve at the Diplomat.

"We had eighteen people at the table," I explained. "Freddie and his broad and Tommy Farese, you know, the Colombo doper. A couple of his lobs. And Jiggs was there with his wife. Jiggs was impressed we had the front center table. Even stars like Jackie Gleason were sitting behind us. I wondered if Sinatra recognized

Jiggs, because he sang to our table for over an hour. He even asked me for some ice for his wine. It was red wine. I guess he wanted to cool it off.

"So, after that, I used to see Jiggs at the track and we became friends. I got him front-row tickets for a Liza Minnelli concert in Fort Lauderdale. He asked me because he said Freddie Campo was making too big a deal over it. I even met Ally Boy through Jiggs."

The capo Alphonse "Ally Boy" Persico was brother to Carmine "the Snake" Persico, boss of the Colombo Family. The mention of Persico's name seemed to wake Tommy Agro up.

"Joey, so you know who Jiggs is, right?" Tommy asked.

"Hey, Tom, I'm just friends with the guy. I don't do business with him," I lied. "I heard he was a capo with the Colombos. I told you that already, Tommy."

"Okay, Joey, calm down, it's all right," Tommy said. "I like the guy a lot myself. He's very well respected, and he knows you're with me. He's a man, Joey, not like some of these other cocksuckers. Joey, you're learning. Just try not to make too many mistakes, because I like you very much."

There was always a hint of menace in the heart-to-hearts I had with T.A. I guess otherwise he wouldn't have been T.A. But the beef between Tommy and me was over with. I could see that. I felt comfortable around him again and was glad. Frankly, I enjoyed being around him. And he liked me because I wasn't a freeloader. I earned. That, and I could handle things for him.

"Joey," he asked, "what happened when you met with my *compare*? Remember he called you from Naples?"

Oh *marrone*, I thought. What a fuck-up that had been! Tommy was talking about Joe N. Gallo, the *consigliere* of the Gambino Family. At Tommy's suggestion, he'd called me from Naples, Florida, a few months before, only Tommy hadn't told me who the guy was. We'd gotten on like oil and water. I told him the story.

"He calls me in the morning, Tom, and tells me he wants to meet with me in an hour. I told him I had business to take care of, but I would be glad to meet with him anytime after four o'clock. 'What's this?' he says to me. 'Some kind of joke?' Then he called me a jackass.

"Well, Tom, you know me. I don't take that kind of shit from anyone, and I told him so. I told him the only reason why I was even talking to him was because my *compare* T.A. says you're close to him.

" 'Close to him,' he screams over the phone. 'You be at the fuckin' Diplomat at seven-thirty tonight! And don't be late.'

"I didn't know what to do, Tommy. That's when I called you. I mean, you didn't tell me who he was and all. You know?"

"Yeah, Joey, I know," Tommy said. He was shaking his head. "He called me and told me. I told him you didn't know anything about him. He laughed. A little."

"Yeah, well, anyway, I show up that night at the Dip," I said, picking up the Gallo story, "and he was waiting there at the valet station. 'Joe Dogs?' he says. 'Joe N.?' I say. And we embrace. He apologizes for calling me names. We had dinner and a few drinks, and he asked me to pick him up the next day and drive him around Naples. Said he wanted to build a house.

"So, since you told him I'm in construction, he wants me to build him the house. But, Tommy, the guy wants a quarter-million-dollar house built for nothing. What the fuck?"

"I know, Joey," T.A. said. "All these zips are that way. They think the world owes them. But, Joey, he's number three in the Family. He's the *consigliere*."

"Wow," I answered sarcastically. "Let me say it backward. Wow. How does that sound?"

"Don't fuck around, Joey. He's a good man."

"Hey, Tom, that's just the way I am. I like people. I don't give a fuck if they don't have a dime. But when people start acting like kings, shit on them. I don't like them. We went to the Calder track while he was here. Did he tell you?"

Yes, Joe N. Gallo had told Tommy Agro about our day at the races. It had been a disaster. Earlier in the year my uncle and I had bought a nag, Elfin Water, and the first three times we raced her she finished eleventh in a ten-horse field. Anyway, Little Dom Cataldo had been down from New York a few weeks before Gallo, and he had talked me into experimenting with this new kind of horse dope that was supposed to be untraceable. The first time they

were supposed to shoot up Elfin Water, she went off at five to one, and I put $1,000 on her to win. She finished last.

Little Dom had called from New York saying he hadn't been able to get to the stable hand. He promised next time would be a lock. I'd put the matter out of my mind. Coincidentally, the next time my horse ran was the day I took Joe N. Gallo to the track. He didn't want to hang out with me, he didn't want to meet my pals. But before we parted in the grandstand he did ask about my horse. I'd told him I thought she "had a shot." No more, no less. I didn't want Joe N. Gallo throwing his good money after my bad.

For loyalty, I put a twenty-dollar wheel on my horse in the daily double. Five minutes before post time she was listed at seventy to one. I went over to the window and put $200 on her to win. She went off at twenty-five to one. I had $400 invested in her. She won by three lengths and paid $52.80. I won a little over $12,000.

Gallo came running over to me after the race screaming that he hadn't bet her. He was pissed off. I left the track after the second race. Back at home, Little Dom called. He'd bet $2,000 with his New York bookmaker for me, to win. He was holding $50,000 for me. I was up $62,000. Joe N. Gallo was out.

"So that's how it happened, Tom," I said.

"Okay, Joey, but my *compare* thinks you didn't let him in on something that you were sure was coming down. He's still really pissed off."

"Tom, you know I'm not like that," I protested. "In my mind, I really didn't believe that Little Dom could do anything. And besides, I told Gallo we 'had a shot.' What did you want me to do? Split my winnings with him?"

"Joey, all I'm trying to say is that Joe's been pissed at you for a long time now. I tried to explain it, but he didn't buy it."

"And another thing, Tom. In my mind I'm not even sure if Little Dom got to the stable hand and shot up the dope. Because after that race the horse ran second twice and won two more times."

"Yeah, Joey, I know."

Tommy knew? How the hell did he know? I wondered.

"We bet her in New York three of those times," Tommy added. "Didn't you get down?"

"A couple bucks at the track," I said. "Tommy, are you trying to tell me that there was something going on with *my* horse and I didn't know about it?"

"Joey, you don't know Dominick like I do," he said. "He made a fortune off your horse."

"I'm sorry, Tom," I told him. "But in all due respect I have to say that I can't believe that Little Dom did that without letting me in on it."

Tommy Agro bared his teeth. "Joey, you're fuckin' dreamin' if you think Dominick isn't going to do something to your horse without your knowledge. Especially when there's money involved."

"Well, maybe you're right, Tom," I said. "But let me ask you this: If there was something going on, how come *you* didn't tell me?"

Tommy didn't answer me. He just looked at me like he didn't know what to say.

Three Points
a Week

Tommy left for New York in early summer 1974, and things got back to a little more normal. I sold Elfin Water to some guy who wanted to race him at Rhode Island's Narragansett Track, but not before I replaced my trainer with a kid named Howie Ruben. The horse never won under Ruben. I think the best she ran was one second and one third. She was hurting anyway—bowed tendons. In hindsight, I suppose my first trainer knew how to take care of a horse and this guy Ruben didn't.

One day I was sitting in the grandstand at Calder down in Miami when Ruben approached, asking me if I'd like to buy "a real good horse cheap."

"The horse has good bloodlines, Joe," he said. "He's out of Forli, the Italian champ."

What the fuck did I know about horses? I knew how to bet them. I knew how to curse when they lost. I knew how to cheer for them down the backstretch.

"How much can you get the horse for?" I asked. "And who wants to sell it?"

"The owner wants thirty thousand for him," Ruben said. "He's a yearling, and he'll be a good stakes horse. Joe, he's really a bar-

gain at that price. These horses go for at least a hundred thousand at the annual Ocala auction. But you know what? I'll tell the owner we'll give him twenty thousand up front, and then the other ten thousand after the horse wins his first race. We'll run him in a maiden allowance, which is a maiden special weight. This way no one can claim him on you."

Ruben had me all excited now. I was really interested, and I showed it (like a jerk).

"Howie, listen to me," I said. "You don't know me, and you don't know anything about me. Before you do any business with me, I suggest, for your own sake, that you check me out. Do you understand me?"

"Joe, I'll guarantee the horse," he said. "I can't do any better than that."

So I bought the horse. I gave Ruben $20,000 in cash, and two days later he showed me our package.

"Isn't he beautiful?" Ruben asked.

"Yeah, what's his name?"

His name was Glorious Request, although Ruben told me I could change it if I wanted. I didn't bother. I wouldn't know what to call a horse anyway. Just as long as he wins.

"Oh, don't worry about that," Ruben assured me. "We're going to do good with this horse. He might even get to the Derby."

I mean, fuhgedaboudit. I felt like King Tut. I got me a horse that's going to the Derby! Hey, this guy Ruben guaranteed the horse, so I had nothing to lose. What the hell did I know? The horse looked healthy to me. He had legs like a linebacker, thick and strong-looking.

I started getting up early every morning and driving to the barn area. You needed a badge to get in, and since I didn't have one, Ruben would meet me at the gate. Like everything else I owned, the horse was in my wife's name. But I couldn't have gotten an owner's license if I'd wanted one. I had at least a dozen pinches on my rap sheet, everything from B and Es to shylocking, although I was proud of the fact that they were all misdemeanors. I had been arrested a year before for felony assault. But I'd pled down and

walked away with a fine. After a few months the guards at the track all recognized me anyway, and I just drove right through.

I'd watch all Glorious Request's workouts. The gallop. The hot-walk. Working out of the gates. The whole bit. In January 1975 the horse turned two years old and I began asking Howie when we were going to race him.

"Joe, he's not quite ready yet," the trainer would answer. "He should be ready for later on in the Winter Gulfstream Meet. Let's get him real sharp."

Meanwhile, Ruben was always bragging about all "the boys" he knew in Detroit, how much they liked him, how they were only a phone call away. He'd mentioned names I didn't recognize—hey, don't forget, I'm the guy who'd never heard of Joe N. Gallo—and, all in all, he was very convincing. I had no reason not to believe him. It really meant nothing to me, other than the fact that my guarantee looked good if things ever came to a head. A sit-down was all it would take.

One morning Howie approached me with a request. "Let me level with you, Joe," he said. "I push a little cocaine here and there, and I need some seed money. Can you front me something?"

"Is there a lot of money in that shit, Howie?" I asked. I knew how much money was in coke. I just didn't want this moron to know that I knew.

"Joe, you have no idea how much," he bragged. "I can turn twenty thousand into a hundred thousand in one month's time."

"Are you a user, Howie?" I asked him.

"Once in a while, Joe. I use it to clear my mind. It makes you feel real sharp, Joe. I'll get you some and try it, okay?"

"Nah, nah, Howie. No thanks. But I will loan you twenty thousand at three points a week, and I don't want to know what you're doing with the cash. You just have the money every week. That's six hundred a week juice. *Capisci?*"

"Gee, Joe, that's a little steep isn't it? Can you make it two points?"

"Hey, Howie, you just told me how much you're going to make off of it. So what do you want to do, eat alone? Three points,

Howie. And don't—and I emphasize *don't*—be late with the payments. And, Howie, I don't want to try any of that shit. My mind is sharp enough."

"No problem, Joe, three points," he said. "We're friends, right? I just need it for a month or so anyway."

"I don't care how long you keep it," I told him. "That's your business. You know the terms, and you know the complications if you don't meet the terms. I mean, you know all those guys from Detroit, right?"

"Yeah," he answered. "But I don't want to bother them with such a small loan." He was bullshitting.

But Ruben paid his juice on time, no problem. I stopped going to watch the workouts, and he met me every week at a coffee shop in Hallandale, just north of Miami. I'd meet with Jiggs while we waited for the horse trainer to show up. Jiggs, who lived near the diner, would walk his mile, eat half a sandwich, and chew on his cigar. Once in a blue moon he'd light it. "Cigarettes will kill you," he'd tell me every time we met. "I know. I smoked them for forty-five years."

The Glass Diamond

Bunny called me at the construction trailer one day not long after I shyed out the money to Ruben in February 1975. She was in a lather. Someone had broken into the house.

"What did they get?" I asked her.

"I think they took your guns."

"Is that all? Did they touch the bowling ball?" Bunny knew what I was talking about. I had about $200,000 in cash stuffed into the bowling bag at the bottom of my closet.

"No, honey," she said. "The bowling ball's still here. Should I call the cops?"

"Yeah, go ahead," I told her. "And don't forget to tell them about how bad you feel over losing your expensive diamond ring and the silverware set. *Capisci?*"

Bunny giggled. "Oh yeah. I loved those things so much." My wife appreciated the way I always thought on my feet, especially if there was a scam involved. She owned an expensive diamond ring but not a silverware set. However, that wouldn't stop me from filing an insurance claim on both. Little did I know that my cleverness would land me in the middle of a shit storm with certain members of the New York Gambino Family.

A few hours later they found the kid who broke into our house. He was a fourteen-year-old from the neighborhood. When they returned with my rifle and my thirty-eight, I asked about the diamond ring and the silverware.

"The kid says he doesn't know anything about those, um, stolen items," the officer told me. The guy was no dummy. He knew exactly what I was doing. "Would you like to press charges?"

"The hell with that," I said. "Somebody must have come in here after the kid left and stolen the expensive stuff. The diamond in my wife's ring was worth ten thousand alone."

"Must have," the cop said dryly and left.

I had insurance with Comine Insurance Company out of Miami. My broker was a guy named Freddy, whose Uncle Nino was a Gambino capo up in New York. So I really didn't foresee any problem collecting on the "stolen" ring. Comine sent me to the Javier jewelry store in Miami, where they "replaced" my wife's stolen ring with what they said was a two-carat $10,000 pear-shaped diamond placed in a beautiful gold setting.

About six months later I needed money and asked Bunny to give me the ring. I'd lost my drywall contract at Century Village because one of my employees had reported me to the IRS, and I'd hired a karate expert to work the guy over. The guy had been hurt real bad, and the head man at Century Village canceled my contract. I guess I was lucky they hadn't known about the no-show jobs and my other tricks or they would have canned me sooner.

"Jiggs, do me a favor," I asked him the next time we met. "See how much you can get for this stone." We were sitting in the Hallandale coffee shop waiting for Howie to come by with his juice.

"How big is it, Joey?"

"It's supposed to be two carats, worth ten grand." I told Jiggs the story behind it.

"I'll see what I can do," Jiggs replied just as Ruben walked through the door.

"Howie, how are you? You're ten minutes late," I kidded him.

He began stuttering, making excuses. He was a nervous fuck. I was beginning to think he was snorting too much of that nose candy. But then that was his business.

"Howie, I'm making a joke," I said. "But be on time next time."

The following week I arrived in Hallandale early to see what Jiggs had come up with on the stone.

"Joey," he said, "this diamond is shit."

I thought he was kidding.

"My guy told me he wouldn't give you five hundred for it," Jiggs went on, and I started to laugh.

"Those cocksuckers in Miami told me it was worth more than ten grand." I had to give those humps in Miami credit. While I thought I was ripping off the insurance company, they were ripping me off. But that didn't leave me any less pissed off.

"Give me their names. I'll take care of it." Jiggs was deadly serious. "Or tell your man Tommy A. about it. He'll straighten it out. Didn't you say Nino's nephew Freddy was in the middle of all this?"

"Yeah, Jiggs," I told him. "But maybe he's not involved. But that's good thinking. I'll call Freddy first and tell him about it. I don't want to bother Tommy with every little thing. I'll take care of this myself."

The next day I called Comine Insurance and got Freddy on the phone. When I explained what had happened, Freddy said that it was impossible, that Javier jewelry was a highly respected outfit. "Are you sure your appraiser is being straight with you?" Freddy asked, and for a moment I felt like scaring him just by mentioning the name Nick "Jiggs" Forlano. But I didn't want Jiggs involved, so I took off on the kid myself.

"What the fuck are you talking about, Freddy? Are you calling me a liar? I'm just telling you what my friend told me."

"Joe, don't talk to me like that," Freddy replied. "I just said maybe your friend made a mistake. I don't appreciate your language."

"Freddy, I don't give a fuck what or what you don't appreciate. Who the hell you think you are? Just get me my ten grand back before I have to take this further than a phone call." I hung up.

About three weeks later Glorious Request was entered in the maiden special allowance race at the '75 Summer Meet at Calder race track. Tommy A. and some of the guys flew down for his

debut. I was a big man with Agro now. I owned a horse, and he owned me. He liked to show me off. Tommy was staying at the Diplomat, and a few nights before the race he pulled me aside.

"Joey, Nino come to me in New York. All he says is 'That Joe Dogs down in Florida is starting a lot of trouble.' Joey, I don't know how to answer him. I don't know what to say. What's going on?"

I told Tommy what happened, and he blew his fucking top.

"I wish you would have come to me with this sooner, Joe," he said. "Because I would have told him to go straighten out his fuckin' nephew. But you know what you do now, Joey? Get in touch with this fuckin' Freddy. Tell him to come to the Dip. Tell him I want to see him. And I'll call Nino and tell him I plan to talk to his nephew."

I called Freddy and gave him Tommy's message. Freddy said he'd have to check first with his Uncle Nino. "Do whatever you have to fuckin' do," I told him. "But be at the Dip tomorrow at two P.M. sharp."

Tommy and I were lounging by the pool the next afternoon when Freddy came sauntering in. He hugged Tommy, said hello to me, and added, "My uncle sends his regards." After a little small-talk bullshit, Tommy got to the point.

"Listen, Freddy, my close friend Joe Dogs here tells me he had an insurance policy with you, and that you replaced a ten-thousand-dollar diamond ring that was lost or stolen or whatever. But wherever you sent him to get it replaced, they gave him a bogus piece of glass."

"Well, Tom, in all due respect," Freddy replied, "Joe here could have changed the stone and—"

"Whoa, whoa, wait a minute here, Freddy," Tommy interrupted. "I'm only showing you this respect because of your uncle. Now, if you want to make accusations that Joe here is trying to swindle you out of a few grand, then, my friend, this conversation ends right here. My advice to you is to get out of here, go tell your uncle what you just told me, and I'll straighten it out in New York."

"Tommy, Tommy, I'm sorry," Freddy backtracked. "I'll tell you

what I'll do. Me and Joe will take the stone to the Diamond Exchange in Miami, and we'll see what they say."

Tommy just looked at the kid. Tommy wasn't one to be fucked with. He played by the rules. He had listened to Nino's beef about me, had gotten embarrassed because he didn't know what it was all about, and had eaten Nino's shit, so to speak. But now he had the picture, and all he saw was some punk kid trying to throw his weight around because his uncle had a name.

"Listen, my friend," Tommy said to Freddy, "I won't tell Nino the way you talked, because he'll rip your eyes out of your head. Just get this thing with Joey straightened out. If you're right, I'll be the first to apologize. But if you're wrong, then pay him the ten grand, no bullshit. I have no more to say, except that I want this straightened out today."

I told Freddy I had the stone with me, and we went to the Diamond Exchange together. But first Freddy told me he wanted to call Javier's and tell them about the stone. This could go either way, I was thinking. Either the kid is trying to show me he doesn't know anything about the mix-up, or he's telling the jeweler what to do.

We arrived at the Diamond Exchange. There were about fifty jewelers in the place.

"Hey, Joe, let's go to this guy over here," Freddy suggested. "Excuse me, we need an appraisal on this diamond."

The jeweler examined the stone with his jeweler's loupe. Turned it around. Measured it. "Well," he said finally, "this stone can be bought in one store for, say, ten to twelve thousand, or in another for, say, eight or nine thousand. Depends on where you shop. Sometimes you're only paying for the name on the window."

Freddy looked pleased. I wanted to knock the smirk off his face.

"Excuse me, sir," I said to the appraiser. "I was told by a jeweler friend of mine that this stone isn't worth five hundred. To be perfectly honest with you, I hope you're right. Because Freddy here is a witness to what you're saying. And I'm going to get another *unbiased* jeweler to give me an appraisal. In the event this ring is not what you say it is, I will subpoena the both of you, and then sue you."

I was bluffing, of course. Freddy knew it. The jeweler didn't.

"Hold on, I don't want to get involved," the appraiser said. "I received a call from someone at Javier's, and they described the markings on this stone and told me to appraise it for above ten thousand. I'm not going to get myself in trouble or lose my license over this nonsense. The diamond is worthless."

"Gee, Joey, you were right. I'll tell Javier's to replace it." Freddy had balls, I'll give him that.

"Forget about the stone," I told Nino's nephew. "I want the fuckin' money. Call them and tell them I'll be there Friday to pick it up."

My horse was running the next day, and I didn't need this aggravation. I explained what happened to Tommy, and he was overjoyed at being able to go back to New York and put Nino in his place.

"I'll tell that fuckin' Nino how they tried to fuck you, Joey, and I'll tell him in front of people and make him look like shit."

Later, Freddy called Tommy and asked if he could have a little time to straighten this out.

A Horse Out of Kelso's Ass

Glorious Request opened at twenty to one. He was running against a field whose owners had paid anywhere from a quarter million to a hundred grand. My horse was the cheapest. Don't worry, I kept reminding myself. He was out of the Italian champ Forli.

It was the winter season, the track was busy, and a lot of money was changing hands. I gave my jockey his instructions. I told him to win. Our workouts had been good, but so had the workouts of just about every other horse in the field.

Glorious Request went off at eight to one. I bet so much money my friends thought I was nuts. I bet with both hands, close to five grand. I think Tommy got down for $1,000, based on my say-so. The rest of the guys were in anywhere from $200 to $500.

They were off. The horse that cost a quarter of a million took the lead. It was a five-furlong race. He reached the quarter pole in twenty-two seconds. Glorious Request was running second, one length behind. The leader hit the half mile in forty-five and three-fifths, which is a pretty fast pace for two-year-olds. Glorious Request was still holding second but losing ground. Seconds later our

race was over. My horse ran dead last. He packed it in after half a mile.

I was stunned, in a daze, when my jockey found me after the race.

"This fuckin' horse wasn't ready," the jockey said. "And that asshole trainer knew he wasn't ready. Glorious Request is a long, long way off."

I looked around for Ruben, who was afraid to come near me. I wanted to choke the cocksucker to death.

Tommy grabbed me and said, "Joe, the horse was right there until the stretch, maybe he just needs a little more work. Give the trainer a break."

I snapped out of it. Tommy saved Ruben from catching a beating, and me from being pinched. Everyone offered their condolences. I talked nice with Howie Ruben. And I left the track $10,000 lighter.

I didn't have much time to fool around at the track. I was hustling like never before. Shylocking. Shakedowns. Bookmaking. I started dealing drugs. The whole bit. Losing the construction contract at Century Village had hit me harder than I had expected. That drywall business had been bringing in over $5,000 a week. I used to have money coming out of my ears. Now I was working every angle I could find.

"Hey, Howie, when is this horse going to win?"

Glorious Request had run four times. The best he'd ever finished was sixth in an eight-horse field. We were running him now in $15,000 claiming races. Of course nobody wanted to claim this dog.

"Howie, my friend, I've already lost over twenty grand because you keep telling me he's ready. So be honest. Is he ever going to win, or what?"

It was six o'clock in the morning. I'd gone to watch the horse work five furlongs. Howie and I were standing by the railing at the main workout track.

"All you wops are alike. If your horse don't win, you blame the trainer. Did you ever stop to think that I have feelings, too?"

Smack. I hit him open-handed, like you hit a broad. He landed on his ass, got up, started to say something while covering his face, and I kicked him in the stomach. I was aiming for his balls, but I missed. He doubled up, and I grabbed him by his hair and began smacking him back and forth, open-handed, like he was a broad.

"Listen, you motherfucker," I hissed through clenched teeth. "You know the twenty thousand I paid for that horse that you guaranteed? And you know the twenty thousand you have out as a loan? And you know the twenty thousand that I lost gambling on this fucking horse? You have exactly seventy-two hours to come up with it. Sixty grand, Howie. I suggest you get in touch with your so-called friends from Detroit. Because if you don't have the money by then, you'll be the sorriest motherfucker alive. I'll be back in three days. Have anybody here you want."

Then I punched him, knocked him out, and left.

One thing I must say for Howie Ruben. He may have been fucked up, but he never ran to the law. Maybe he was just too afraid of the consequences. I really didn't expect him to get up the money, and there was no way he owed me my gambling losses. I had merely lost my temper. But just in case, when I drove out to the track three days later I took three of my crew along, in the event that there was a problem. We all had guns.

At the gate the guard stopped me and asked who my friends were. I told him we were thinking of forming a racing syndicate, and they were potential partners. He let us through, no problem. We drove to the area where I had worked Howie over, and there he was, waiting alone.

I got out of the car. He was trembling.

"Easy, Howie. Easy. Nothing's going to happen." I motioned to my crew to go for coffee at the track cafeteria, and Howie visibly relaxed.

"Joe, I couldn't come up with that much money. All I could get was thirty thousand. I had to go to a guy who loans you money on your home. Will you give me more time to come up with the rest?"

"Howie, look," I said. "Number one, I'm sorry I smacked you

around, but you shouldn't have talked to me the way you did. Number two, you don't have to pay for my gambling debts, but you did guarantee me the horse, and I'm going to hold you to it.

"So give me twenty thousand for the horse. And if you want to give me the other ten thousand for the loan, then you only owe me ten thousand and your juice payments are three hundred cheaper a week "

Howie said, "Joe, let me give you the twenty thousand, but hold on to the rest. I want to buy some of that stuff, you know what I mean? And I'll keep paying the six hundred a week interest."

"Whatever, Howie. It's up to you. It's your loan."

"And, Joe," he said, "the horse is still yours. You don't even have to pay me to train it. We'll drop him down to a five-grand claiming race and win a big bet, and then the purse will be yours."

"Fine, Howie, fine, whatever you say. But I'm not sure if that horse could win if he was the only one in the race," I said. "And, oh, by the way, I never paid you for training that horse anyway. That was part of our agreement."

"Oh, yeah, Joe, I forgot. And Joe, one more thing. If my wife asks you, will you tell her I gave you all thirty thousand?"

I shook my head in disgust. "Yeah," I said.

I called Little Dom in New York and told him about my horse. I was thinking about what those drugs had done for Elfin Water. He laughed and said, "Joe, there's nothing you can do with that nag."

"But Dominick," I protested, "we're dropping him down to five-grand claimers. And he's out of Forli, the Italian champ! We should win here with a little of that happy juice."

"Joe, I don't care if he's out of Kelso's ass, that horse don't win. Let me explain it to you, Joe. Remember when he finished sixth. You asked me to send in a G on him to win? Remember?"

"Yeah," I said.

"Well, Joe, I didn't want to tell you, but I bet five thousand to win and five thousand to show, because we did that Elfin Water thing on him, you know, and the best that crippled fuck could run

was sixth. I wanted to fly down there and get the horse and the trainer and chop both their heads off."

I started to laugh and said, "I already gave the trainer a beatin'. And I let him give me back the money for the horse. He's a coke freak and into me for twenty large. But he's as good as gold with the juice. I wish I had ten guys like him."

"That's good, Joey." Dominick laughed. "But keep him in his place. Listen, I have to go now, but I'll be calling you in about a week. You know that guy at the Bridge Restaurant in Fort Lauderdale? You know who I mean, don't you? I don't want to mention his name on the phone."

He was talking about Tommy Farese, the Colombo doper who had sat with us at Sinatra.

"Yeah, Dom, I know who you're talking about. Why?"

"Are you in good with those guys? Because they're with, uh, my, you know."

Dominick was telling me that he and Farese were with the same Family.

"Dom, you're not telling me anything I don't know. And to answer your question, yeah, they love me. I can get anything I want from them. Why?"

"Good, Joey. I'll let you know next week," he said. "I'll talk to you then."

Miami Ice

It had been over a month since I'd heard from Freddy, my top-notch insurance agent. I called him.

"Freddy? Joe Dogs. Howya doing?"

"Fine, Joe, fine. I was just talking to my uncle about you the other day. I was going to call you."

Freddy couldn't say two words without bringing up Uncle Nino. He thought that the name would send shivers down my spine. "Well, do you plan on taking care of your obligation, or do I have to go further?" I asked. "You've had enough fuckin' time."

I didn't care how I talked to this pimp.

"Listen, Joe, why don't you and I go to Javier's tomorrow? I think you'll be satisfied."

"I can't go tomorrow," I told him. "You call that Jew bastard and tell him I'll be there at one-thirty Friday afternoon." I hung up without giving him a chance to come up with an excuse.

Friday came. I picked up my juice from Ruben in Hallandale and mentioned to Jiggs that I had business at Javier's. Jiggs offered to ride along, which I appreciated.

"I know that cocksucker in Javier's," he told me. "If he sees me, he'll shit his pants."

Jiggs and I walked into Javier's Jewelers separately, with Jiggs walking to a corner, pretending to be window-shopping. He was carrying a small fishing gaff under his coat. He told me that if anyone gave me a problem he'd be more than happy to rip their

eyes out. I walked up to the counter and signalled to the guy who had originally given me the stone. There was also a woman behind the counter, and I could see a little jeweler working in a room behind the store.

"Here's your piece of glass, you crooked fuck."

"Don't talk to me that way," the guy said. "Who do you think you are? I'm going to give you six thousand for that ring, and that's all."

The woman came and stood next to him. And the worker from the back came out, too.

"Listen, cocksucker, all of you listen. You give me ten grand, and if I have to wait more than five minutes for it, you're going to pay me five points juice, retroactive for the last eight months. And you have one other thing coming."

I reached over, grabbed this fuck by the tie, and backhanded him. He started bleeding from the nose and mouth. Just then Jiggs appeared at my side. "Hi, Joe," he said amiably. "You having a little problem here, or what?"

"No, Jiggs, I don't think so. My friend here has a nose bleed and I'm trying to tell him what's good for it."

The clerk recognized Jiggs, nodded hello, ran back to his office, and came back with a $10,000 check. "I left the name blank," he said. "I didn't know what name you wanted to use."

I said, "Listen, take this check and get one of your flunkies to cash it right away. I want cash. *Capisci?*"

He went back to the office, returned with the cash, and ordered the salesgirl to bring me a solid gold bracelet. "Keep it, with our compliments," he said.

On the drive back to Hallandale I slipped Jiggs $1,000. He didn't want it, but I insisted. He thanked me. We both went to the track. And won.

I mailed Tommy $2,000 and told him what I had done.

"Did you get me a bracelet, too?" he asked over the phone.

"No," I said, "But you can have this one. I saw some fag wearing one just like it. So it's all yours, buddy."

"Keep talking with your fuckin' mouth that way, Joey, and I'm going to sew it up." He laughed.

Part Two

The Player

"I'll Kill Her Mother and Father!"

I'd been a member of T.A.'s Gambino crew for four years now. In spite of Tommy's warnings, I was double-banging him behind his back. It just didn't seem right that I could only earn from one *Famiglia*. It was undemocratic. I was forty-five years old and invincible. So when Little Dom Cataldo called me in early 1976 and wanted to know if I could score him some pot, I didn't think twice about doing business with the Colombos. The Gambinos always looked down at the Colombos anyway, like they were junior members of our mob. And it's a fact that they did a lot of Gambino dirty work. Most Colombos were crazy. So I felt like I was working with distant relatives, though I knew Tommy wouldn't have seen it that way.

"I need about five or six hundred pounds, Joey," Dom said. "But don't let them know it's for me."

Tommy Farese would front me as much pot as I wanted. I had a good name with him. Besides, I rented a storage warehouse in Riviera Beach, one town over from West Palm, for his *com-*

pare, John "Johnny Irish" Matera, whenever they brought in a load.

"Fine, Dom, should be no problem," I said. "But who you going to send to pick it up?"

"I'll send Billy Ray down, and he'll drive it to the Auto Train, like that, you know." Billy Ray was part of Little Dom's crew.

The next day I met with Farese and his partner, Harry Roth, and ordered a carload. I had a big trunk and back seat. They loaded the car with 580-odd pounds of Colombian Gold. I told them I'd have their money in two or three weeks.

"Joey, there's about ten extra pounds in there," Farese said. "But you owe us for five eighty at one thirty. Comes to seventy-five four. Make it seventy-five even. Okay?"

"Yeah," I agreed. "I'll get it to you as soon as possible."

"Don't worry, Joey, we trust you."

"Hey, Dom," I said into the receiver. "Call me at this pay phone from outside right away." I gave him the number.

I never had to pay for long-distance calls from pay phones. I had a gadget that made sounds like quarters, dimes, and nickels dropping into the slot. It fit right into a Marlboro cigarette box, and all you had to do was press the buttons on this little machine next to the speaker on the phone. It was a great little gizmo. They still use them to this day.

Dominick called me back. "You got the stuff?"

"Yeah, a little over five eighty. We owe them seventy-five G's. I told them two weeks. Now, Dom, this stuff is Colombian Gold, so don't take no less than three dollars a pound, you know what I mean?"

By three dollars, of course, I meant $300. "It cost me one thirty. *Capisci?*"

"Very reasonable," Little Dom replied. "We're partners, Joey. Okay? And do me a favor. You're down there already, so rent a car and load it up. Cover the stuff with some blankets. I'll have somebody pick it up in Lorton, Virginia. It'll save us a world of time."

"No problem, Dom. I'll call you, then you call me back outside,

and I'll get you the make and the color and the plate numbers and everything."

I got one of my crew to go to someone he could trust and rent the car. The precautions may sound confusing, but I was just layering myself from the law. We picked up a four-door Buick and I sent one of my guys as a mule to drive it to the Auto Train and meet Dom's guy in Lorton, Virginia. When he hooked up with Billy Ray I had him call me, and I spoke to Billy myself to confirm he'd picked up the load.

Dominick was very pleased. "This stuff is dynamite," he told me over the pay phone. "I think I can unload the whole shipment in one place, maybe for a little cheaper. What do you think?"

"I don't know, Dom," I answered. "If you're going to price it out piecemeal, get four hundred a pound. If you're going to let it go all in one place, don't let it go for any less than three hundred a pound."

"All right, Joey, fine. I was just asking."

"Dominick," I said, "just do what you think is best. I'm not going to question your judgment. Whatever you do is fine with me. Just get me seventy-five thou as soon as possible."

Little Dom promised he'd fly someone down with the money in a few days. "You can't mail that kind of cash," he added.

Before he hung up, I mentioned to him that Tommy Farese had thrown in an extra ten pounds. "In case you want to impress some broad, Dom," I said.

"Nah, Joey, that don't work," he said. "They want candy—the snow. It gets them crazy." He hung up.

I thought it was time I gave my wife and kids a break. We all went on a trip to Disney World. The kids were super happy. Bunny was ecstatic. I had become a lousy husband. I was never home, always out gambling, or bedding down with some broad. And I had added jai alai to my gambling lust. I used to go down to the West Palm Beach jai alai arena, sit in a private room, watch the games on closed-circuit television, and bang the hostess. I also banged two of the waitresses. I mean, I had become a real whoremaster. I was

even beginning to disgust myself a little. I'd meet a broad, spoil the shit out of her, take her to bed, and then move on.

Bunny was very suspicious, forever accusing me of fucking this one or that one, and as much as I denied it—"Who do you think I am, King Kong?"—I knew she just knew.

In fact, she turned into something of a detective. Once she even tailed me to a broad's apartment. Knocked on the door, came crashing in, and went after the broad with a knife. *Marrone*, what a fucking scene! I grabbed the blade and cut the hell out of the palm of my hand. Then I carried her out kicking and punching all the way. She was, that is.

I made her feel terrible. It took her two weeks to forgive me after that one. I swore on the Bible I wouldn't do it again. I took her away for a weekend then, too. To Naples, Florida, to a nice hotel. I gave her the salami all weekend, and she seemed to be happy. But she never trusted me after that. She checked up on every little thing.

"Bunny, honey," I'd plead. "I swear I won't do it anymore. So give me a break, will you? I can't take you every fuckin' place I go."

I felt like a prisoner.

Dominick called. "Where the fuck you been? I been trying to reach you."

I told him about Bunny catching me with the broad and the make-good weekend in Naples.

"Joey," he said, "I get caught all the time, and when my wife threatens to leave me, I tell her to go ahead. I tell her if she leaves me I'll kill her mother and father."

"You crazy bastard," I said, laughing. "I can't do that. Bunny's mother and father are already dead."

"Don't worry about it, Joe," Little Dom said. "Where's she gonna go with four kids? Anyway, the reason I called is because of that, uh, you-know-what. I'm at a pay phone. Here's the number. Go out and call me back."

I left and called. "What's up?"

"I let that shit go for two eighty-five," Dom said. "One guy, the

whole shipment. It's over with. I got a hundred sixty-five grand. You give those guys their seventy-five thousand and we make forty-five grand apiece. You want some extra for the car rental and the blankets and shit?"

"You calling me petty now, Dom?" I kidded. "Go fuck yourself."

Little Dom told me he'd arranged for one of his crew, a gorilla named Ralphie, to fly down with $120,000, Tommy Farese's money plus my share. "Don't pay him, I already did," Dom added. "Just get him a hotel room and a broad."

"Are you kidding?" I said. "Where am I going to find a broad to sleep with that big ugly fuck? He looks like Godzilla."

"Sorry, Joey," he said. "I already told him you had a nice blonde lined up for him."

Dominick gave me Ralphie's flight number. He was landing in West Palm at eight-fifteen that night. I was at a loss. I knew this animal would go nuts if I didn't get him a broad. Then a light bulb went off over my head. Ruben always had a lot of nice-looking broads working the backstretch. Hotwalkers. Exercise girls. Work-out girls. They were a different breed of people. They were also, most of them, young and good-looking. Howie used to fix me up with one every now and then. I called him.

"Howie, I got a friend who just got out of the joint. I need a nice looker. A blonde. I'll pay two hundred."

I went home and told Bunny what was going on. She was incredulous. "You're kidding? With Ralphie? Oh, the poor girl." Two hours later Howie called from the lounge at the Holiday Inn. I met him at six-thirty, two hours before Ralphie was due in. He was sitting with a gorgeous young blonde. She was just beautiful.

"Joe, meet Janice. She's one of my better workout girls. And she just loves Glorious Request."

"Yeah?" I said as I shook her hand. "She can have him."

I ordered a round of drinks, reimbursed Howie for the room he'd taken, and began explaining the facts of life to Janice.

"Look, honey, this guy you're going to meet looks like something of a rugged individual," I told her. "But he's a nice guy, a real pussycat. He's been away for a long time, so do me a justice and be

nice to him. He's going to fall in love with you when he sees you. He's a good close friend of mine, and whatever service you perform will be well rewarded."

Janice was insulted. "I'm no prostitute, so don't hand me any money," she said. "I'm just doing this as a favor for you and Howie. What I'd like in return is to work out your horses."

I'd recently bought a couple of cheap claimers to keep Glorious Request company. "Honey," I said, "if anyone else but you ever gets on my horses in the morning, you just give me a call and I'll have a little heart-to-heart with Mr. Ruben here."

Howie left, and Janice and I had another drink. She told me how Beverly, another workout girl, had told her what a nice guy I was. She was making me feel like a heel, and I wondered what Bunny would think if she walked in. Nonetheless, I was hoping Ralphie's plane crashed. I really dug this baby doll.

Soon it came time to pick up the moose. I didn't want Janice to go to the airport with me. I wanted to speak to Ralphie alone. That Dominick, I thought on the drive over, he's doing this just to break my hump.

Ralphie was waiting for me in the lounge. He was wearing a real tourist outfit, right down to the checkered pants. Too bad he didn't wear a mask.

"Ralphie, baby, how you doing?"

He only carried a small bag. He was just staying overnight. Thank God! "Hey, Joe, I thought maybe you forgot about me. Where's the broad?"

"Just hit some traffic, Ralphie, sorry. She's waiting at the Holiday Inn. She's already got a room. And she's dying to meet you."

"Is she nice, Joey? Is she blond?" he asked.

"Ralphie, she's gorgeous and she's blond. Now listen to me, be nice to her. I told her you were a good friend of mine, and I told her you were a real nice guy. So don't be mean to her, and don't hurt her."

"I won't hurt her, Joey," Ralphie said. "No way! I just hope she'll do what I want."

"Yeah, she'll do anything," I said to him. How the hell did I know what he wanted her to do?

When Janice sweetly introduced herself to Ralphie I would have done anything to trade places with that big lob. They made small talk about the weather and about Ralphie's flight down hitting turbulence and about whatever, and I had to get out of there. I couldn't take these two lovebirds anymore. When I told them that my wife and I were going to a late dinner, I thought I saw a shadow of disappointment cross Janice's face.

"My plane leaves at eight-fifteen in the morning," Ralphie said. "Do you want me to take a cab, or what?"

"No, I'll pick you up at six," I told him. "Janice, here's my phone number in the event you have any problems."

Ralphie went to the bar to pay the check and I gave Janice a quick kiss and left.

"How did the girl look?" Bunny wanted to know.

"Eh, she was a little fat. You know, nothing I'd look at. But too good for Ralphie."

"She can only stay with him until midnight. She's got to leave because she's married," I continued lying. "They aren't staying at the Holiday Inn. I took them downtown."

"How is she going to get home?" Bunny didn't miss a trick.

"She'll call Ruben, I guess," I said. "But I gave her our number in case she has any problem with that animal."

Bunny wasn't quite convinced. "I hope you don't have to take her to Miami."

"Hell, no," I said. "That's Ruben's problem."

Bunny bought it. I was glad. I mean, I hadn't done anything wrong anyway. And after a night with Ralphie, there was no way I'd touch that broad now.

"I have to get Ralphie at six-thirty in the morning," I told Bunny. "Take him to the airport, then I'm going to the track to watch the workouts. You want to come?" I knew she didn't.

"No, honey, you know I don't like that Ruben. Does he fool around on his wife?" She smiled. "You know, like you do."

Bunny was a pretty lady, a good mother. She had a lousy husband. Could I help it if I liked girls?

. . .

The phone woke me up. It was five-thirty in the morning. A sweet voice said, "Hi! Don't forget to pick your friend up."

Bunny had opened her eyes and was looking at me.

"Sure, Ralphie, no problem, you got plenty of time," I said. "Let me grab a shower, then I'll be right over."

"Oh, gee, Joe, I'm sorry," Janice replied. "I forgot about your wife." She hung up.

"I thought you were supposed to wake *him* up," Bunny said suspiciously.

"I guess he's nervous about making his plane."

I showered as quickly as I could, worrying like hell that Ralphie would call back. He didn't. When I arrived at the hotel room, Ralphie was packed and dressed, checkered pants and all. Janice was splayed out nude, asleep on one of the beds.

"She wants you to come back and take her to Miami," Ralphie said on the drive to the airport.

"Did you enjoy her?" I asked. "Did she do what you wanted?"

"Joe, she was great," he said. "She did everything I asked her to. I left her five hundred. I put it in her purse because she didn't want anything. I'd like to see her again."

"Okay, Ralphie, only let me know a week ahead of time next trip. Tell Dom to give me a call." I dropped him off, parked my car at the airport lot, and took a cab back to the Holiday Inn. I didn't want Mrs. Sherlock Holmes to spot it at the hotel. I had Ralphie's key, and when I walked through the door Janice was sitting on the bed, nude, soaking her hands in a bucket of ice. I didn't ask.

Janice looked at me—a little sad, I thought—and took her hands out of the bucket. They were red and swollen, especially her right hand.

"What the hell happened?" I asked, and she began laughing hysterically, laughing so hard it was catching. I began laughing too.

"Joe, after you left, Ralphie and I came to the room and un-dressed," she said. "To be quite frank, he was built pretty good, too. He says to me, 'Joe told me that you'd do anything I wanted.'

I was a little apprehensive. I didn't know how to answer. Finally I asked him exactly what it was he wanted. 'I want you to spank my ass real hard while I jerk off,' he says.

"So I told him I'd never done anything like that before, and he'd have to show me what he meant. 'Like this,' he says, putting me over his knees and smacking my ass. It hurt. I didn't like it. But he told me he wanted me to smack his ass real hard."

Janice began laughing again and put her hands back in the cold ice bucket.

"So, he gets on his knees," she continued. "And I start to smack his ass. He's yelling, 'Harder! Harder!' as he's masturbating. I did that for at least forty-five minutes, and then he shot his load all over the sheet and went to sleep."

Janice looked up at me with a smirk. "Different strokes for different folks," she said, breaking up again.

"When Ralphie woke up, he wanted his ass smacked again. He came faster this time. I guess I'm becoming a professional ass beater. At any rate, it made me a little horny, Joe. You interested?"

I looked at her and wanted her. Wanted to make love to her. But something held me back. Something was wrong. I don't know what it was. I just sat down next to her and we fooled around for an hour, kissing and hugging. But I didn't fuck her.

After Janice showered and dressed she found the $500 in her purse. She tried to give it back to me, but I told her she'd earned it and made her keep it.

"Glorious is running today," she said. "I'm going to parlay it on him. Howie told me he's going to win."

I looked at her and said, "Oh yeah? Give me that money. I'll bet it for you. When you get to the track, go around and tell everyone Glorious Request is going to win today, okay?"

"Sure, Joe, but won't that make him the favorite?"

"Listen, Janice, just do like I say and don't ask me any questions."

I stopped the car on the way to the track to call Little Dom. We had a lot of time. Glorious Request wasn't running until the third race.

"Joe," he reminded me, "that nag of yours is running today. He

ain't got no chance, and I got a 'friend' with a horse in that same field. You want down on him?"

"Yeah, Dom, give me five nickels on the front end of the car." My usual bet with Dom was $2,000, or four nickels.

"Fine, Joe," Dom said, adding, "but please don't bet him at the track. The odds, you know. And how come five nickels today?"

"Because I'm in love and one of the nickels is for her."

"Don't let Bunny catch you again," Dom warned with a laugh. "Did Ralphie give you the bazookas?"

"Yeah," I replied. "I had Ralphie taken care of. He's a sick guy, Dom. Did you know that?"

"Yeah, Joe, I knew," he said. "I wanted you to get a laugh. All the guys around here are a bunch of sickos."

We said goodbye.

It was near post time for the third race, and Ruben was dressed in a suit. He thought he was going to get his picture taken in the winner's circle with Glorious Request. Janice had done a good job touting him, and she asked me if I'd bet the $500 for her.

"All on the nose," I said.

Then I went to the window two minutes before post time and wheeled Dominick's "friend's" horse in a twenty-dollar perfecta, as this wouldn't affect the odds. He went off at four to one.

The race was over. Dominick's horse won. A twelve-to-one shot ran second. Glorious Request may still be running. The perfecta came back $168. My twenty-dollar bet paid $1,680. Janice was devastated.

"Janice honey, er, I made a mistake at the window," I said. "I bet the three horse instead of the five horse. You won by mistake. You won twenty-five hundred. Honest, here's your money. I even won by mistake myself. But let's not tell Howie. Let him think we lost."

"Why?" she wondered.

"Because that's what I want sweetheart. Don't go against me."

"Joe," she said, "I think I could fall in love with you."

"Honey, don't do that. You'll get over it."

I left her at the track and went home.

All Fucked Out

I had bet $2,500 with Dominick, so I had $10,000 coming from the book in New York. But my mind was really screwed up now. I felt like I was falling in love. Christ, I thought, this can't be happening. I'd been married for twelve years. I had four kids. It wasn't rational. Plus, and it was a big plus, this was 1976, still back in the Stone Age when the big shots in the Mafia didn't look kindly on a man leaving his wife. Girlfriends were one thing. But second wives were usually young, stupid, and likely to get a gangster in trouble. I had to figure this out in my head. I didn't go near the track for a month, and I didn't answer the phone for anyone except Little Dom and T.A.

But Janice never called. I don't know if that made me glad or unhappy. Ruben called every day, however, wanting to know where I was, wanting to know where he should make his juice payments. Finally, I drove to Hallandale to meet with the horse trainer.

"Where the hell you been?" Jiggs asked. "Ruben's been going nuts. He didn't know who to give the money to, so I took it for you. Here." Jiggs handed me $2,400.

I told Jiggs I'd had a personal problem and I'd been laying low. Then Ruben came in.

"We got a big problem, Howie," I busted his chops. "Jiggs tells me he asked you for the money and you refused to give it to him."

But Howie didn't fall for it. He was smiling. Jiggs said goodbye, and Howie and I talked.

"That girl Janice is crazy about you," he began. "Why don't you give her a break. All she does is pout. She won't even work out your horses. I told her I was going to have to let her go. She even came down here with me the last couple Fridays hoping to see you."

"Let me tell you something, Howie. If you fire that girl, I'll break both your fuckin' legs. And I'm not kidding. And if she comes down here every Friday, how come she's not with you now?"

Howie was still smiling, the dopey fuck, when he said, "She's in the car waiting for you."

I was so happy I threw Howie a hug and went out to get her. Janice was in tears. "What's wrong?" I asked.

"It's just that, Joe, I've been sitting out here so long that I thought maybe you didn't want to see me," she said. "I knew you were here. I saw your car. All the other times I'd never seen your car, and Howie wouldn't allow me to go inside because he said he met with your uncle."

Ruben rose a notch in my estimation with that. I didn't think he was that sharp.

I said, "Come on, Janice, get in my car. We're going away for the weekend."

Howie walked out and she began to protest, saying it was her weekend to work. She needed, she said, Howie's permission.

"What the hell's wrong with you, Janice?" Howie said. "You want me to catch a beating? Take off three weeks, with pay. And if you need three more, take them, too, with pay."

I laughed like hell, and so did Janice. All the way to Key West. We checked into a beach resort but never left the room until checking out Monday morning. Janice wanted me to leave my wife and kids. As I dropped her off at the track Monday morning, I tried to set her straight:

"Look, honey, I care for you, and if we stayed together I could even fall in love with you. *But*. I'm sorry to say this, but I don't think you should bank on a future with me. My wife and children mean everything to me. I'm only being honest with you. There's no sense in leading you on. I'm sorry, honey. Goodbye."

It was too bad. But that's the way these things happen. On the drive back to West Palm I started to laugh, thinking that the one who was going to suffer the most was Ralphie. Who was going to spank his ass now?

When I pulled into our driveway, Bunny came running out of the house. "Joe, what happened? Where were you? Are you all right? You look terrible."

How else would anyone look who had fucked themselves silly for three straight days?

"That's a multiple question," I said sarcastically. "Which one do you want me to answer first?"

"Never mind," Bunny said accusingly. "T.A. wants you to call him. He was worried about you *also*."

Tommy and I had worked out a code, where if I ever had to lie to him over the phone and wanted him to know it, I'd call him "Tipperino." I was hoping he remembered.

"Tipperino," I said into the receiver. "I've been kidnapped since Friday. There were three guys. I think they were with the Colombos."

"You cocksucker," T.A. said with a laugh. "You had us all worried. I hope it was worth it. Is she nice, you bastard?"

"Tom, I got away beautifully, the best thing I ever did in my life. But they left me in bad shape. They were kicking me in the balls all weekend."

"Sure," Tommy said. "You're all fucked out, and you can't take care of the wife. Call me tomorrow. We need to talk." He hung up the phone.

Bunny had been standing right behind me. It was building in her, and she had to let it out.

"So what is she? Blonde? Brunette? Redhead? You bastard!"

"I had one of each," I shouted at her. "I fuck them all. That's what you think anyway, isn't it?"

Then I punched my fist through the bedroom door, unplugged the phone, and went to bed.

The Big Fix

"Hey, Tom, what's up?" I said into the phone.

"Listen, Joey, get down to the Gulfstream racetrack. Go to the restaurant in the clubhouse. Ask the maitre d' to point out a guy named Sean O'Leary."

"Why?" I asked.

"Hey, Joey," Tommy Agro growled, "you better stay out of the sun and stop fuckin' around with the broads and start tending to business. I say go see the fuckin' guy. If I tell you over the phone, the whole fuckin' world will know! You idiot!"

He was right. I wasn't thinking. I'd called him at his house from my house. Who knows? Either one of us, if not both, might have been bugged. Anyway, I was sure I already knew why. I'd lay five to one that it had something to do with fixing a race. We were always fixing races. If only the public knew how easy it was to reach jockeys and trainers and hotwalkers. I mean, the track was made for the mob. The '76 Winter Meet at Gulfstream was just about to begin, and I had no doubt Tommy was sending me to set up a scam.

"Yeah, okay, Tip, I'm sorry. I just woke up."

Tom said, "Get down there today. He's waiting for you." So I drove to Gulfstream in Hallandale and the maitre d' took me to Sean O'Leary.

"I'm Joe Dogs," I introduced myself. "I haven't the slightest idea why I'm here. T.A. says you'll explain everything."

Sean O'Leary didn't strike me as a mick. In fact, he didn't strike me as much of anything. He gave new meaning to the term nondescript, the kind of guy who could lose a tail in an elevator.

"Joe, you'll need between forty and fifty thousand, and we can fix a race and cash in on it" were the first words out of his mouth. "That will be the initial investment. Of course, that covers all expenses as well as bets. We can continue to do this throughout the whole meet. I couldn't do it at Calder because I was told by Matty Brown Fortunato that there's already an outfit out of Kansas City that runs things down there."

"Matty Brown" Fortunato was a New York–based capo in the Genovese Family.

"And it can't be done at Hialeah because the stewards are too sharp," Sean O'Leary continued. He pointed to a race on the Gulfstream card. "If you have that kind of money on you, we could fix this here field today."

In fact, I did have that kind of money on me. But I wanted this "fix" explained thoroughly to me. I wanted to know how he intended to do it, the risks involved, exactly who was in on it, the guarantees, and, of course, how much money we could make. Then I would have to talk to T.A.

But I was excited. I loved nothing better than a sure bet.

BETTING. Most people know how to lay two or five or even a hundred dollars on a horse to win, place, or show. It's the so-called exotic betting, the perfectas and trifectas, that confuses their minds.

To bet a perfecta at a horse or a dog track, there must be at least five entrants in the race. In the perfecta, you are betting that you can pick the horses that will finish first and second, in that order. Usually that bet will cost you two dollars.

But say you wanted to "box" four horses in a field of ten, that is, bet that any two of those four horses will finish one-two. That will cost you more. Here is how you figure the cost if the mutuel is

a two-dollar bet per perfecta, which it is at most tracks. In this case, the bet would be on four horses. You take the next lowest number, which would be three, and multiply four times three. You have twelve. Then you multiply that number by two. So you'd have to put up twenty-four dollars to "box" four horses. Or say you wanted to bet five horses "boxed." Multiply five times four and get twenty. Then multiply twenty by two. It will cost you forty dollars to "box" five horses, and eighty-four dollars to "box" seven horses. (Figure it out.)

Now a trifecta is a little different, because your entrants must finish first, second, and third, in that order. There must be at least six horses running to bet a trifecta. A straight trifecta bet also usually costs two dollars. I have no cute multiplication table to explain trifecta "boxing," but the track supplies a table showing you how much it costs to "box" any amount of horses in a trifecta. To "box" three horses will cost you twelve dollars, or two dollars down on every conceivable finish those horses could run. A four-horse trifecta "box" costs forty-eight dollars, and so on.

And finally there's the "wheel." When you're "wheeling" a horse or dog, you're essentially betting a perfecta, with the rest of the field covered. In other words, in a twelve-horse field, if you feel certain that, say, the seven horse is going to win, you can bet the rest of the field to finish second for two dollars a horse. Wheeling a trifecta costs a little more. The track usually provides a betting chart on how to wheel a trifecta.

There are also more exotic bets like the "back wheel," where you can bet on one horse finishing second and the rest of the field finishing first, but I think that's enough of a lesson for today, eh?

Sean O'Leary was explaining the scam.

"Joe, the involvement and risks to you guys are minimal. I know the jockeys I can approach. This is done early on the morning of the race. Once I pay a jock to pull and finish no better than third, he's obligated to do so. The only risk involved is an unforeseen act of God. There's nothing I can do about that. However, I will personally guarantee the money otherwise. If there is a double-cross, I

pay the money back within thirty days at a reasonable rate of interest. No shylock juice, though.

"So this is how it goes," O'Leary continued, pointing to the program sitting in his lap. "Say there's a nine-horse field, like this race going off next. There are five jockeys I can reach in this race: the one, the two, the five, six, and nine. I've used these jockeys before. This happens to be a high-priced claiming race. I will never approach an apprentice jockey, that's asking for trouble. Anyway, it would cost about twelve grand to fix this race. Look, the favorite is opening at eight to five. It'll take three grand to pay off that jockey.

"This one," he said, pointing, "will cost another three grand. This other horse is five to one. That costs two grand. And the other two I can probably get for fifteen hundred apiece. That leaves four horses—and four jockeys—that are medium prices to longshots. So now, we have to box them in perfectas only. That'll cost us twenty-four dollars per bet.

"So, what we want to do is box them four hundred times. Our total bet would be ninety-six hundred. Then take the change, say four hundred, and throw it on a wheel or two on the slim chance you'll hit it. That makes a total of ten thousand bet, plus eleven thousand for the fix, for a grand total of twenty-one thousand.

"So let's say a twenty-to-one shot wins, and a thirty-to-one shot runs second. Now normally that perfecta would come back paying probably over a thousand to one. But being that we've bet it four hundred times and driven the odds down, let's say it pays, oh, three hundred and twelve dollars.

"We would get back a hundred twenty-four thousand and eight hundred dollars! And if we got lucky and hit the other four hundred on wheels, we could wind up with another ten to twenty grand. Do you follow me so far, Joe?"

I looked at this man. I didn't know much about him. But right now he looked like Santa Claus to me. This wasn't a beat. This was serious stuff.

"Sean," I told him, "let me get back to T.A. with this. Then I'll get back to you."

"Fine, Joe," he said. "But try to be here with the cash on Satur-

day. That's the biggest handle. And tell Tommy I want an equal share for my part, with no investment."

"Okay, Sean, an equal share with no investment. But you're also holding the guarantee alone," I reminded him.

"That's right," he answered. "But tell Tommy that on some days we're bound to get an eight-horse field, which means we get to five jockeys, box the other three horses, only bet ten to fifteen grand, and maybe wind up with a hundred fifty grand."

"I'll tell him, Sean. I'm interested. I'll probably see you this Saturday."

The more I thought about it, the more I liked Sean's plan. I knew I could come up with the money on my end. And I knew Tommy could on his end. But would he? I rang him in New York and told him to call me back at a prearranged outside number. The pay phone rang and I went over the scam, explaining everything in detail.

"And he said he would stand behind the money?" T.A. asked when I was finished. "And he knows that when he guarantees this thing, that if he don't keep his word, it's like telling God to come and take him?"

I laughed and asked, "What do you want to do? Sean says he needs forty or fifty large. Send me your end, I'll put up my half, and we'll split three ways."

"Send my end," Tommy spit out. "Are you crazy, Joey? This is my thing. You're only in it, my friend, because I'm trusting you to watch out for my back. But better yet, listen. You know that banana-nose Freddie?"

He meant Freddie Campo, the bookmaker. Of course I knew him.

"Go see him and tell him I sent you," Tommy said. "Explain everything to him, and see if he'll put up the bazookas."

"I could do that," I said. "I'll tell him we'll guarantee the money."

"No, no, Joey. Not like that. Tell him me—Tommy A.—guarantees the money. And tell him we split four ways. Tell him how good a deal it is. He'll go for it."

I told Tommy I'd be in touch and hung up. He had a phone

beeper like I had, so it never cost him any money to call long distance. Fuck AT&T.

I had no idea what T.A. had in mind when he told me to see Freddie Campo. Freddie had most of the bookmaking action in Palm Beach County, and he wasn't affiliated with any of the Families. He didn't want to pay rent to anyone. That was nice when you were making it. But on the other hand, if there was ever a problem, Freddie had no one to run to.

When I explained the scam to Freddie, he jumped in with both feet. "If Tommy guarantees the money, I'm in. But I'd like to hear it from him."

This skinny, ugly cocksucker was doubting my word. I was just about to answer him when he said, "On second thought, Joe, your word is good enough for me. I don't even want that fuckin' animal to have my phone number."

I started to laugh. Tommy Agro had some reputation. "Don't worry, Fred, I won't give him your number. So do you have the fifty large? We need it by Saturday."

"*Marrone,* I know I'll have forty grand. Will that be enough?"

"Yeah, that's enough," I said, figuring that if we came up short I'd cover the rest.

I got in touch with Sean and told him it was a go, and that I'd be at Gulfstream on Saturday by noon. He said that if there was a race he could fix, he'd need a minimum $10,000 to $15,000 to pay the jockeys up front, just so there would be no mistakes.

"No problem," I told him. "See you Saturday. Oh, and by the way, Sean. Now it's a four-way split. We got another partner."

That's all I told him. I didn't go into detail with him, because it was none of his business. As far as he knew, he was playing with T.A.'s money, and that was that.

"Joe, I don't want to meet the other guy," Sean said.

"Sean, and he don't want to meet you. In case anything goes wrong. Do you understand me, Sean?" That last was a none-too-subtle reminder to Sean about who he was dealing with.

"Yeah, Joe. See you Saturday at noon."

Santa Claus Meets the Mob

Sean had a fix in the sixth race, a ten-horse field. It was a cheap claiming race for three-year-olds and up, horses which hadn't won more than two races in their careers.

He told me we'd reached five of the ten jockeys, and he broke down the payments, for a total of $9,000. He could have told me it was costing $15,000 to fix the race and I never would have known the difference. So he was being honest, as far as I could see.

"Box the remaining five four hundred times," Sean told me. "This way, we'll take down most of the pool."

"Okay, Sean, that's five horses boxed. That's forty dollars per box, times four hundred. We bet sixteen grand." I thought for a moment.

"Why don't we do it six hundred times," I suggested. "It'll cost us twenty-four thousand. I have that kind of money with me."

Sean liked the idea. Then he gave me a warning.

"Don't approach me at all for the rest of the day. We'll meet at the Diplomat tonight, in the Celebrity Room, and divide the winnings there."

Little did Sean know that nobody was going to be dividing any "winnings" until the end of the sixty-day meet. That was the plan

T.A. and I had come up with. We'd pay back Freddie's original investment, of course, but I'd keep everything else until we played out the scam.

I met Freddie in the lower grandstand and pointed out Sean, who was hanging out in a different area of the track. Now Freddie knew what Sean looked like, but Sean didn't know Freddie. That was just in case things didn't happen according to plan. Freddie could take care of Sean. Tommy and I had given this responsibility to Freddie. Whether he did it himself or farmed out the job, we didn't care.

"Here's the numbers, Fred," I explained. "Go to the second floor and wait until the sixth race. Go to the ten-dollar window and get in line about five minutes before post. Try and time it so you hit the window maybe two, three minutes before post time, so no one but the clerk will think anything's up. Hand the guy the numbers on a piece of paper and tell him to box them three hundred times. That's twelve thousand bucks' worth.

"Hand the money up front to the clerk, and he'll punch his heart out. I'll do the same down here. We'll meet back here after the race. I hope this is no fuck-up."

Freddie looked at me and went his way.

The sixth race came and we had the five horses with the shortest odds fixed. None would finish any better than third. Barring an unforeseen calamity—Sean's act of God—we would bang out the perfecta.

I reached the ten-dollar window with just under three minutes until post. The clerk began punching out on that machine and ten-dollar tickets are flying out and the people on line behind me are beginning to shuffle their feet and mumble. With one minute left to post, they began yelling.

"Hurry up, you motherfucker, we're going to get shut out."

Fifty-five seconds to post.

"You should die of cancer, you rotten bastard."

With fifteen seconds to spare I walked from the window with a paper lunch bag brimming with ten-dollar tickets. In those days the tracks weren't equipped with computers, and the highest perfecta ticket you could bet was ten dollars. Today, you can bet $100,000

on one ticket and any moron can punch it in. But before computerization, it took a fast clerk to take care of big bets like ours.

Post time. We'd bet the one, two, five, nine, and ten horses.

The nine horse won at eighteen to one. The two horse, a twelve-to-one shot, ran second. The exacta paid $382.80. Multiplied by 600, our return was $229,680. Minus the payoffs to the jockeys, and the $24,000 we'd bet, our profit came to $196,680.

"Fred," I said, "go cash your tickets in with the guy you bought them from. Give him a couple hundred for himself. Spread four or five hundred around the rest of the clerks, because then they'll work with you easier."

Back in the 1970s you could bet all you wanted and get paid back in cash. Today a lot of tracks will only give you a check if you win more than $10,000. Not all, but a lot. They say it's for your protection, that they don't want you to get robbed. But I'd rather take my chances in a track's parking lot than with the IRS.

After our windfall, Freddie and I drove to the Diplomat, where we met up with Sean. Freddie could show his face now, because we'd made our seed money back and there was no cause for alarm. I gave Sean the lay of the land.

"Freddie gets his up-front money back, and I hold the rest," I told him. "Tommy says that no one gets any money until we're all through. He told me to let you have fifteen thousand for the next fix, in advance. And he expects it to happen at least once a week. I just got off the phone with him, and he told me to send you his regards and remind you to behave. Do you have any problems with that?"

"Joe, I owe money to shylocks and bookmakers," Sean whined. "I told them I'd pay them today. Could you let me have at least five thousand so I can pay off my juice?"

"Sean, look, I'm only following orders. I'll tell Tommy to call you. In fact, let me call him right now. I'll be right back."

"Tom, Sean needs five grand for some orange juice," I said over the phone in what passed for our half-assed code.

"Give it to him," T.A. replied. "Because I'm the fruit peddler that he's buying the oranges from."

"You fuck," I told him, "you're collecting from all angles."

"Hey, Joey, what did you think? That I was made with a finger? Give Sean the bazookas, and tell him to see me in a few days. I'll have his oranges for him."

Actually, I didn't want to say anything in front of Freddie, no sense him knowing Tommy's business. Tommy agreed. I gave Sean the money. Freddie picked up the dinner tab. And we left. On the way out Freddie thanked me for cutting him in, and I rolled him some figures.

"You got your up-front bazookas back, I gave Sean twenty grand, we spread eight hundred around the clerks, so that leaves us with $175,880. That figure coincide with yours, Fred?"

"Yeah, sure, Joe. No problem."

I got home early for a change and Bunny jumped on my case. "What's wrong?" she asked. "You got stood up? Or did you finally decide to give me and the kids a break?"

Somebody Gets Whacked

By early '76, things were back to normal, and despite the collapse of my drywall business I was doing good. I had a nice bookmaking operation. I had this thing going at the racetrack. My shylock customers were all paying on time. And I had been doing a little drug dealing with T.A. and Little Dom. Separately, of course. That's where the real money was, in drugs. All in all, I figure I was taking in between $200,000 to $300,000 a year, tax-free, with about 10 percent of that being shipped north to my *compare*, Tommy Agro.

Of course, I could never hold on to a buck. Nobody in the organization could. We all threw our money around. Broads and more broads. Lawyers for pinches, bondsmen for bail. The lawyers got the most, though. We called them whores. They got that name for jumping from one client to another. I had a good lawyer. I got sentenced to a month one time. He got me out in thirty days.

But I loved the life. Of course, not everything about being a gangster was as pleasant as fixing a horse race. Sometimes you had to kill people. I hated that part of it. Well, maybe not hated it, but when it happened I could never eat my dessert after dinner.

. . .

"Joe, wake up. It's Dominick on the phone." Bunny's voice brought me out of a nice dream involving Janice.

"Tell him to call back later," I groused. "I'm too sleepy to talk to anyone."

"He says it's important."

"Son of a bitch. . . . Hello, Dom. What's up?"

"Wake up, Joey, I'm flying in tonight," he said. "Pick me up in Fort Lauderdale at nine-fifteen. I'm on Delta. You got to do something for me. I can't come dressed, so have some clothes for me and for you. *Capisci?*"

Dominick Cataldo was telling me he couldn't carry a gun on the plane. He wanted me to secure us a couple. I didn't know what the hell was coming down. Since when, I wondered, did I start taking orders from the Colombos? Even a good friend like Little Dom, who I didn't mind working with when it was on my terms, knew I was loyal to the Gambinos. I'd been a member of T.A.'s crew for nearly four years now. What the hell was the sense of paying rent if every New York mafioso could call up and order me around like a Florida buck private?

"Joey? Joey? You hear me? Are you awake, you fuck?"

"Yeah, yeah, Dom, I hear you. But you better call Tommy and get his okay first. I don't want to get caught in a swindle. You know what I'm talking about?"

"I'm one step ahead of you," Dominick replied. "I already went to him. And he says for you to help me, with his blessings."

"Hey, Dom, that's not what I meant," I lied. "I'd do anything for you, you know that. But if I did something without telling him and he finds out, well, you know what a fuckin' animal he is. What size jacket do you want me to bring?"

"I wear a thirty-eight," Dom said. "And listen, you know those slacks you got for my girl? She has a twenty-two waist. Bring them, too."

"Okay, Dom, I'll see you tonight." I hung up.

What the fuck did Dominick want with a thirty-eight pistol and

a twenty-two pistol? I'm sure I'll find out, I thought as I fell back to sleep.

I picked up Dominick and we drove south. He handed me an address in the Keys.

"I got to see a couple of Colombian guys," he said. "You wait in the car. Did you bring the guns?"

I had. Two snub-nosed thirty-eights and a little twenty-two. Dom took one thirty-eight and the twenty-two and stuffed them into his waistband.

"Dom, what the hell is coming down?"

"It's nothing, Joey," he said. "I just want to talk to these guys, is all. I just need the two pieces in case they don't hear so good. I'll only be a couple of minutes. In fact, you don't even have to turn the car off."

I found the place. Small ranch house–cum–fishing shack nestled inside a shadowy cove of bougainvillea.

"Go around the block and park," Dom ordered.

As I backed the car up, Dominick put on a long blond wig. Then he covered his face with a black beard and mustache.

"You go ahead," he said. "Drop me off on the corner, and after I go in, pull up in front of the house with the lights off and the car running. Don't ask no fuckin' questions."

I didn't. I dropped him off and he minced up to the front door like a fag. I watched him enter, and once he got inside I began to pull up the car. I heard about twelve shots. Dominick came walking out and hopped into the passenger seat.

"Let's go," he said. "Take me to Miami Airport and then go home."

On the drive north he told me that a "couple of spics" had beaten him and his *compare,* the Colombo capo Allie LaMonte, out of $80,000 on a dope deal. "I needed the disguise in the event someone else was there," he added. "It's a good thing, too. There was a broad and two young kids."

"Dominick! You didn't?"

"Naw, Joey, I don't hurt kids or women. But without the dis-

guise, I wouldn't have had no choice. Christ, I'm hungry. Where can we get a quick sandwich?"

He just whacked a couple of guys and now he was hungry. Sometimes I couldn't believe the people I was hanging around with. We stopped for a sandwich at some Cuban joint and then drove to the airport. On the way I drove over a bridge and Dom dumped his two pieces into the Miami River. After I dropped him at his airline gate, I headed straight for the Diplomat. I needed a drink. I went to the Tack Room and caught the last show, met a good-looking chick, and spent the night in a suite. I always got a room dirt cheap. They gave me convention rates.

The Big Fix II

I called Bunny the morning after Dom whacked the Colombians, and she relayed a message from Sean. He needed me at the track today, with $30,000. I gave Freddie the word, and we met at twelve-thirty. Sean had already taken care of the jockeys, reaching five in the nine-horse field for the third race. All we had to do was box the other four horses.

"Get them four or five hundred times," Sean said, which annoyed me.

"Hey, Sean, don't tell me how many times to get them," I said. "I know what to do."

On the way to the betting window I ran into two friends, legitimate people, Gerry and his lovely wife, Glenda. I advised them to put a twenty-dollar box on our four horses, without telling them why, and then hooked up with Freddie. I gave him the numbers on our race.

"Let's get them six hundred times," I told Freddie. "It's a twenty-four-buck box, so that'll cost us fourteen four. I got thirty grand on me, so let's wheel and wheel back for another eight hundred each. Here's eight grand. You know what to do. I'll meet you at the Dip after the race. Let's not be seen leaving the track together. I don't want anyone to clock us."

Just as Freddie was leaving, Checko Brown, a Colombo made guy, came rushing over to me.

"Tommy told me what's going on," he panted. "Give me the numbers."

"I don't know what you're talking about," I said.

"C'mon, Joe, give me a break. I just want to get down a ten-buck box."

"Checko, there's nothing happening today, so keep your fuckin' mouth shut. *Zitto! Capisci?*" I turned away and left.

I left the clubhouse and went into the grandstand, where I ran into Gerry and Glenda.

"Joe, these horses look like dogs," Gerry said. "Are you sure?"

"Gerry, don't ask me no questions," I said. "I'm just doing you a favor. Now hit it, and stay the fuck away from me, and don't mention it to no one."

The third race went off, and I had the one, four, five, and eight numbers boxed. I'd wheeled the one horse 300 times just for fun. The eight horse finished first and paid twenty-five to one. The five horse placed and paid three to one. I collected $39,600. Freddie should have had the same, unless he hit a wheel.

I tipped the clerks $600 and left the track with $39,000. At the Diplomat I met Freddie. He'd hit his wheel and picked up an extra $13,000. On two races we'd pocketed over a quarter of a million dollars. I called Tommy and told him and he was content. And I assured him I'd let him know the next time Sean got in the fix. I knew Tommy, he'd get impatient soon and start with the phone calls.

Then I told him about Checko Brown and asked why he couldn't keep his mouth shut.

"That's all we need is to let the Colombos in on this," I said into the pay phone. "He'll tell everybody. You put me on the spot today, Tom. I had to lie to a made guy."

"Well, Joey," he said, "I was testing you. Now I'll tell him not to bother you. But it wouldn't have hurt to get a bet down for him."

"No way, Tom," I answered. "I don't like the fuckin' guy to begin with. And if Sean finds out, he'll fuck us around."

"Okay, Joey, but I think you're making a big thing out of nothing. Checko's a close friend of mine, and I wanted to make him a

few bucks. Him being with another *Famiglia* doesn't make him a bad guy."

By now I was remembering that this whole deal was Tommy's. And if T.A. wanted to help Checko out, who was I to stop him.

"Listen, Tip, I'll tell you what I'll do," I said. "The next time Sean calls and we do the thing, I'll put a twenty-dollar box in for Checko, without Freddie or Sean knowing. Then I'll give him his winnings and tell him it's from you. Okay?"

"Good idea, Joey," he said. "But you could tell him the gift is from you."

"Nah," I told T.A. "I don't like the guy anyway. We'll see what kind of mood I'm in."

"Tell him whatever you want, Joey." He laughed. "But take a Midol before you go see him. It usually helps my girlfriend when she has her period."

"Go fuck yourself, Tommy. And thanks a lot for renting me out to Dominick, you bastard. Next time *you* call me and tell me to pick him up at the airport. Not him, or anyone else. You call me! *Capisci?*"

He said goodbye and hung up.

A Favor for
the Boss

Four weeks went by, and Sean fixed five more races in the '76 Gulfstream Meet. On two of them we must have taken down the entire pool. I was holding over $800,000, and Sean was going nuts. He wanted his end. But Tommy said no.

"If you don't give me my share, I'll quit," Sean threatened one day.

"Tell the fuckin' mope to quit," Tommy told me. "Then he don't get nothing."

When Sean got a little too loud with his threats, Tommy had to fly down and slap him around. There was nothing Sean could do about it. But even Freddie was getting antsy, wanting his cut.

I asked Tom again.

"No. Wait," was all he said.

Tommy was speaking into the receiver. "Joey, you got to come in. I have to talk to you up here. My *compare*—you know who I mean, the number three?—he wants you to do something. I can't get into details over the phone, so fly in tonight. Try and make it LaGuar-

dia. And bring three hundred large with you from our corporation."

He hung up without letting me respond. And I had a date that night with a gorgeous blonde. But I had to go. There was no explaining anything to that lousy bastard, much less his *compare*, the Gambino *consigliere*, Joe N. Gallo. Yet in a way I was proud of myself. In just a little over four years I'd gone from a Florida freelancer to attending midnight meetings with the Gambino Family bosses. I mean, I had management potential.

I arrived at LaGuardia at nine forty-five that night carrying an extra change of socks, shoes, shirt, and suit, as well as a money belt strapped to my waist holding $300,000. I couldn't help but wonder why he wanted the money. We had spoken briefly about the four of us taking $150,000 apiece and leaving the rest in the "corporation." So he was due no more than $150,000. Oh well, I was sure he'd have a good explanation.

"Joey, over here. What the fuck took you so long?"

The plane had vectored for close to an hour, trying to find a hole in the thick New York fog. "I was up in the clouds, Tom, wondering whether or not to come down with all of this money."

T.A. smiled. We embraced. We got in his car.

Driving toward Brooklyn, Tommy asked for the money. I took off the belt and handed it to him. "There's three hundred large there."

"How much you got left over?" he asked.

"A little over five hundred large," I answered.

"Here's what you do," he said. "Give Sean his hundred and fifty grand. You take your one fifty. And what will that leave you with?"

"About two twenty large."

"Okay," he went on, "give Freddie the twenty grand, and don't tell him anything else. I'll tell Sean to say nothing. The rest we'll keep gambling with. I'm making my *compare* a partner, Joe. It will be good for your future. He's still pissed off at you from that last time at the track. Tell Freddie we're all just taking twenty grand apiece."

"Look, Tom, as far as I'm concerned, I'm giving you Freddie's

end," I told him. "I don't give a fuck what you do with it. And as far as Joe Gallo goes, I don't care what you tell him. He's got no reason to be pissed off at me. And I don't give a fuck if he is or not."

Tommy pulled the car over to the curb. He turned to me and said nice and calmly, "Joe, do you know what you're saying? Are you that fuckin' naive? You don't think this guy will have you killed in an instant for thinking things like that, much less saying them out loud?"

Tommy was screaming now. "You got to be real stupid, Joe. Now I'm going to tell you for the last time: Don't be disrespectful about him, not even in front of me. Because I'll hurt you, Joe. And I mean it. The guy is like a father to me. Do you understand me?"

"*Minchia,*" I said. "Take it easy, Tom. I'm only talking to you. I'll show the guy a world of respect. I'm sorry. It won't happen again.

"Forgive me?" I teased.

"All right, Joey, you fuckin' fink." He laughed. "Just remember, I warned you. Now listen, my *compare*'s got a girl, a young girl, down in Naples named Sophia. She's nineteen; maybe twenty, and they fool around a little bit now and then. But this Sophia's got a brother who's giving her trouble. He slaps the shit out of her. My *compare* wants him fucked up. He wants him hurt, Joey, but he doesn't want him dead, *capisci?*

"And it's gotta be done when she's up here with him. He don't want no fuck-ups, and he don't want anyone to know. Joey, we don't even want you to use your own crew. I told Gallo you could take care of it professionally, so don't disappoint me. I repeat, Joey, do not let me down on this."

Neither of us said another word until we got to Brooklyn, where we were supposed to meet Gallo. But he'd left word to meet him instead at the Skyway in Queens. The Skyway was a motel with a nice restaurant and lounge, always a good band playing. Joe N. Gallo didn't go there too often. He preferred the young broads in the hip Manhattan disco Regine's.

We arrived at the Skyway, embraced our "hellos," and kissed on

the cheeks in the usual Sicilian ritual. We were not fags by any means. It was just our way of showing respect.

"How have you been, Joe?" Gallo asked me.

"Fine, Mr. Gallo. It's nice to see you. How's your health? You look in great shape."

"Joe, has Tommy told you why I wanted you to come in?"

"He explained," I said. "You need something done, Mr. Gallo, I just want you to know that I'm at your disposal for anything—and let me emphasize the word *anything*. I cannot make it any clearer than that."

"Thank you, Joe," he said. "Now just make sure you do it right. Don't let anything come back to us. *Capisci?*"

I nodded, we embraced again, and Joe Gallo left. Tommy walked him to his car. When he returned, he ordered dinner for two, "the pasta special with the fish, and tell the chef it's for T.A." Then he gave me the particulars regarding Sophia's brother. His home address, where he worked, even a snapshot.

"Get a couple of niggers to grab him and take him to Alligator Alley," he said. "Dump him there. Give the niggers five hundred apiece if you have to. Get them from Miami. Make sure it's a rented car, under a phony name, and do it good. No fuck-ups. If you're caught, you don't know nothing. *Capisci?*"

"No, Tom, if I get caught I'm going to tell them you sent me," I said sarcastically. "Now who's talking like a moron? I mean, you have to say something like that to me?"

"Okay, Joey, I didn't mean anything by it. It's just a habit I have. But don't tell them nothing if you get caught anyway," he said with a smile.

"This pasta is good with the fish," I told him.

"Joey, they treat me like this everywhere I go. In Queens, Brooklyn, Manhattan. I don't give a fuck where it is—I'm always treated this way."

He wasn't lying or bullshitting, either. Wherever I went with Tommy, they would stand on their heads for him if he wanted them to.

.   .   .

I have a vivid memory of Tommy Agro from 1972, back when I first met him. He'd invited Bunny and I to New York for a visit. We stayed in his mansion in Kew Gardens, Queens. The counter-tops and floors were all marble. His master bedroom was one thousand square feet. He gave the room to Bunny and I the night we stayed.

That same night he said to me, "Joey, would you and Bunny like to see Rich Little tonight? He's at the Waldorf-Astoria."

He called at 8 P.M. to make the reservations. "Hello, Pepi? It's Tommy A. I'm coming in tonight. Hold my table. Yeah, yeah, I'll try to be there. If not, we won't be too late."

We left his house at 8:50 P.M. Drove to Manhattan after he made two stops. We were still in the car when I asked him what time the last show began.

"Ten o'clock, Joey. Why?"

"Because it's ten-fifteen now. We're going to miss most of the show."

"We're almost there," was all Tommy said. "We'll be there in ten or fifteen minutes."

Bunny and Tommy's wife, Marian, were talking in the back seat, having a nice chat and oblivious to time. We pulled into the valet parking area of the Waldorf, and the attendants ran over as if they were expecting the Pope. Before we reached the show room the maitre d' was escorting us through the lobby. He nearly had a heart attack when Tommy stopped to get cigarettes.

"Tommy, please," wailed the little French maitre d'. "It's nearly eleven. I'll get your cigarettes, you take your seats."

We walked into the room through one of the fire-exit doors near the stage, and the place was enormous. It was packed with people, except for one tiny table right in front of the stage. That was Tommy's table. We were rushed to our table with everyone staring at us and making snide remarks. We sat down. And then the show began.

I mean, I couldn't believe it. Rich Little had been held up an hour until Tommy "T.A." Agro arrived. Now, drinking in the Skyway Lounge four years later and having just promised a favor to the third-ranking member of the Gambino *Famiglia,* it all made sense.

. . .

"Okay, Tom, I'll leave tomorrow, and whenever you want me to take care of that thing for your *compare,* you call me and consider it done. This pasta's fantastic. I know it's homemade."

"Are you kidding, Joey? If the chef gives me anything but freshly made, he knows he's going to catch a beating. You're going to stay in a good hotel in town tonight, Joey. And don't pay for the room like you did last time. Just sign my name for anything you want."

"*Marrone,*" I said. "How many joints you got up here? Fuck, I'm going to move back to New York. All I got in Florida is a bunch of cockroachy motels and old people. They ride around on bicycles, like a convoy, with a flag flying on a long stick. And if you're driving your car behind them, you either got to run them over or poke along behind them until their leader pulls them off the road."

Tommy started to laugh and said, "That's just your speed, Joey, so be happy with it. You can't move back here. You're stationed down there, and don't ask me why. Just do as I'm telling you. Besides, you got it made and you know it. Hey, Joey, let me ask you something, and I want the truth."

"Tom, don't start with that shit about truth and all that bullshit with me. You got something to ask or say, do it. What the fuck do I have to hide? What the fuck do I have to lie about?"

"Yeah, well, okay," he backed off. "It's about our friend, the little guy. Dominick. When you drove him around that time to the Keys, did he tell you what he did?"

I recited the story for Tommy from the start. When I got to the part about Dom prancing into the house like a fag, Tommy laughed. "You get a hard-on?" he asked. But I ignored him and went on.

"So finally I bring him to some Cuban joint. He gets a sandwich and some of their coffee. You know, like espresso only thicker, and he tells me those two spics had it coming. That they fucked him and his *compare* out of eighty large."

"Did you ask him anything?" Tommy wanted to know.

"Naw, I didn't say a fuckin' word," I told him. "You don't have

to be a brain surgeon to know what went down. I kept my mouth shut and dropped him off at the airport. Then I went to the Dip and spent the night with some chick."

"You see, Joey, let me explain something to you," Tommy said. "The little guy wasn't supposed to say nothing to you, or let you hear anything. I told him I'd let you go with him, but you weren't supposed to know anything about it."

I started to interrupt, but Tommy cut me off. "Wait a minute. Let me finish. It's got nothing to do with trust. If he gets a quirk in his mind and starts to worry that you know something about him, he'll whack you in a second. Do you understand me now?"

"I see, I see," and I did. "Do you think he's worried about me?" I asked.

"No, no, Joey, don't get paranoid," he said. "I talked to him already. Told him I did him a favor by letting you watch his back. Told him to forget all about it and that you had no idea what went down. Told him you never even mentioned word one of that business to me, which Little Dom is sure to take as a sign that you're close-mouthed."

"Remember what I told you over the phone," I said to Tommy. "Don't farm me out to no one else. Don't have anybody calling me telling me to pick them up, or do this, or bring this, or any of that bullshit, and have them say it's all right because T.A. said so. You call me and tell me yourself. Not them."

"Joey, you're one hundred percent right. What can I say? Except it won't happen again. Could you forgive me, darling?"

"Go fuck yourself, Tom. And take me to a hotel. I want to get an early flight out. And one more thing, Tom. I didn't see you give Gallo that money. Are you sure you're not just going to keep it for yourself?"

He was starting to do a slow burn when I told him I was just breaking balls. "Now how do you like it, your word being doubted?"

Tommy smiled and said, "Joey, slow down. You're learning too fast."

He dropped me off at the hotel and blew the horn. The desk clerk came running out. Tommy said something to him, and the clerk

brought me to a room. I entered to meet two beautiful, young girls drinking champagne. They were both naked as jaybirds.

Meanwhile, I was thinking over what Tommy was doing with Freddie's money. I didn't like it, and Freddie knew something hinky was going on when I handed him the $20,000.

"How come we're only taking this much?" he asked. "You're holding a lot of money, Joe. I hope Tommy hasn't got anything on his mind. I was there for you guys when you needed me. And, Joe, I was there for you when you needed me in court."

Freddie was reminding me of the time he'd stood up for me after we'd pistol-whipped some asshole in a restaurant down in Boynton Beach. The guy'd insulted Bunny, and we used his head for a Ping-Pong ball and our thirty-eights for paddles. Coincidentally, by the time assault charges were brought against us, Freddie was already in the middle of a one-year stretch for bookmaking.

He came to court in prison grays and made a deal with the prosecutor to take an extra six months on his sentence for the assault—to run concurrently with the bookmaking time—and I walked out of court with a $500 fine. Freddie was a stand-up guy; not literally Mafia-connected, but stand-up.

And he was right about this payout thing, too. It was hinky. Plus, I didn't like the idea of that asshole Joe Gallo getting Freddie's money. I didn't like it at all what Tommy was doing to Freddie. But I couldn't say or do anything about it.

"He Said He Knew a Hitman"

By 1976 I was well known all over South Florida as a sort of court of last resort. And my reputation as a slugger was only enhanced by my affiliation with the Gambino Family. So it didn't come as a big surprise when one of my shylock customers named Marty Petro called me and told me a lawyer was trying to find me. People were always calling me out of the blue to solve their problems. I was a good problem solver. In this case, the attorney's name was Roberts, and he was a partner in a firm out of Boca Raton. I made an appointment to see him.

"Joe, I represent an elderly couple, very close friends of mine from New Jersey, and they'd like to meet you," Thomas Roberts began. "I told them all about you, and you can probably earn some big bucks from this. There's one thing I have to say up front, though. Whatever you earn, I want half. I don't care what you have to do, but I want fifty percent of whatever you receive."

I was looking at this Thomas Roberts like he was an idiot. I couldn't believe what I was hearing. Does the Lord really put peo-

ple like this guy on the earth? I wondered. But I decided that before I broke his fucking head I'd find out a little more about what he was talking about and, most important, how he found out about me.

"Thomas, let me ask you a question first, if you don't mind me being inquisitive," I said. "How did you come to know about me? You don't have to tell me if you don't want. But if you don't want, this conversation is ended."

"Marty Petro told me about you, Joe," Roberts said. "He said he knew a hit man."

I started to laugh. "A hit man? What the hell is a hit man?"

"Well, Marty said that you could take care of anything. That's why I wanted to meet you and introduce you to this couple. They're very close to me."

Right, I thought. They're so close to him that he wants to earn off them! But I kept my mouth shut. And as for Marty Petro, all he knew about me was that if he didn't pay his vigorish on time, he'd get smacked around. Marty Petro had once seen me kick the hell out of a friend of his who'd been late with the juice. But I never had to lay a finger on Marty. Other than that, Marty Petro didn't know me from Adam.

That's how people are, though. You say hello and they feel like they've known you all their lives when they don't even know your last name. But this guy Roberts had me intrigued with his hint of a big score. I decided to meet his clients.

"Joe, my name is Christopher Woods and I'm from Ridgewood, New Jersey." The speaker was an older man, maybe mid-sixties. Nicely dressed but not flashy. A little reserved, looking a touch scared, as a matter of fact. The kind of guy that's got "Good Christian" written all over him and is wondering what the hell he's doing riding in the passenger seat of a car belonging to someone like me. I figured I'd ride with him just a little longer before getting rid of him.

"Here's my problem," Christopher Woods continued. "My daughter Carolyn's husband was killed in an automobile accident

back in 1971. She received a substantial amount of money from the insurance policy, and—"

"How much did she get?" I interrupted.

"A quarter of a million dollars," he continued. "And they had about fifty thousand saved when he left this world, God bless him. Well, my daughter was despondent, almost dormant, for two years. My wife and I finally talked her into going on a cruise while we took care of her daughter, our grandchild, who was three years old at the time.

"Carolyn sailed on a two-week cruise. It left from Florida, and when she returned she was ecstatic. She said she'd fallen in love with an entertainer. His name is Joseph DeMarco. We hadn't seen Carolyn this happy since her husband was alive.

"Carolyn was determined to marry this man, even though we protested vehemently. Despite our daughter's happiness, my wife and I both thought this romance was a little too 'whirlwind.' I wish she would have listened to us. We wouldn't have this problem now."

The old man was getting off on the story now. "Yeah, yeah, go on." I said. "I don't have all night." I was an impatient bastard.

"Well, they got married two and a half years ago, and he has made my daughter miserable. He beats her occasionally and is extremely jealous of her. He's spent all the insurance money, as well as her savings. He works as a car salesman for Buick now. And I must get my daughter away from him."

"So why don't you do that?" I asked.

"Because Joseph threatened to kill us. He said his father was the New Jersey boss of the Mafia, and he could have anyone killed."

I was laughing to myself. Anybody with an Italian last name was in the Mafia these days! That's what people would believe, anyway. The New Jersey boss! Hah! That *Godfather* movie made it tougher on all of us.

"So, okay, Christopher, what do you want me to do?" He was steering me past the house in Deerfield Beach, halfway between Miami and West Palm, where his daughter and son-in-law lived.

"I want you to beat him up bad enough so he won't hurt my daughter anymore."

"Okay," I said. "But you know he's going to retaliate and maybe come to New Jersey and hurt you and your wife. Then he'll take Carolyn back with him, probably beat her, too, and then we'll be right back where we started. Do you want to risk that? I can't be a baby-sitter for your family for the rest of my life."

We began to drive through the neighborhood where his daughter lived, and Christopher started crouching down in his seat. He was nearly under the dashboard.

"Sit up, Christopher," I told him. "Don't be afraid. So he sees us? What's he going to do? I'll run him over with the car."

I was starting to feel sorry for this old guy. We drove by the house a couple of times, trying to get a glimpse of someone. They lived in a nice residential neighborhood. A duplex apartment. No one appeared to be home. I drove Christopher home.

On the ocean side of Deerfield Beach, Christopher owned two— not one, but *two*—condominium apartments right on the beach. One on the fifth floor and one on the top or ninth floor, facing the ocean. The guy had big bucks.

"Well, Christopher, what have you decided?" I asked him after I pulled into a parking space.

"Joe, you're absolutely right," he said. "I can't risk having Joseph retaliate against my family. The only thing to do is rid him of his life once and for all. But won't there be an investigation?"

"Not if there isn't any body," I answered. "Who would know? But that's expensive Christopher. Do you have any idea what something like this is going to cost you?"

He muttered and moaned for a while, finally asking, "Would it cost about a thousand dollars?"

I looked at him, smiled, reached into my back pocket, and pulled out a wad of hundred-dollar bills. "Christopher, there's about eight grand here. That's my walking-around money. I wouldn't even beat him up for that parsley sum."

"Well, how much would it cost." He didn't say it like a question. He said it like a statement.

Truthfully, I wanted to get rid of this guy and his whole problem. So I said, "Sixty thousand dollars." He didn't blink an eye.

"Wait right here," he said after a minute. "Walk to the end of

our hallway. There's a balcony there. I have to consult my wife."
We were on the ninth floor.

"Christopher, I don't want to meet your wife," I told him. "And
I don't want to discuss it in front of her."

I lit a cigarette and waited on the balcony. Five minutes later a
little old lady appeared, like a ghost. She couldn't have been more
than four feet eight inches tall.

"Are you Joe?"

"Uh-huh."

"Do it. We're flying back to New Jersey tomorrow. Give us a day
to raise half the amount to pay you upfront. The balance we'll pay
after the job's done. All I want is your word that you won't rip us
off for the thirty G's."

I stared until my cigarette burned my fingers. At one time, I
thought, this broad had to be a street person. She certainly talked
like one.

"There's no beat here," I said. "Let's not discuss any more. Send
your husband back out here now, please. Alone." I only wanted to
talk to these people one at a time. If I spoke to both of them, it
could place me in the middle of a conspiracy, and these two could
one day corroborate each other's story in court about any crime
committed.

"I understand," she said and walked off.

"Christopher, are you sure you know what you're getting into?"
I asked when her husband returned. "Once you start, you can't
back off. I mean, a handshake is like a contract."

Christopher understood. He gave me his home number in Jersey
and told me to call him. He'd have, he said, the $30,000. I could
pick it up at my leisure. Then I left.

On the way home I stopped and called Little Dom. "Call me
from the outside right away." I waited ten minutes and the pay
phone rang. I gave Dominick all the details, and there was a brief
silence on the other end of the line.

"Jesus, Joey, sixty large!" he finally said. "How did you come up
with that figure?"

I explained to Dom how I was just trying to get rid of the guy,
but he hadn't batted an eye.

"You should have said a hundred, then." Dom laughed. "He probably would have went for that, too. The only problem, Joey, is that if we do it, what about the people? You want to whack them, too? It doesn't sound like you want to do that, too. But you're definitely going to have to whack that guy Thomas Roberts, because he wants half the money.

"I don't believe these fuckin' people down there," Dom continued. "They must bake their heads in the sun. Anyway, look, pick up the thirty large tomorrow, then take a cab to Queens. I'll meet you at the Palmer Avenue joint. You know the hotel. I'll be in the lounge, say eight-thirty, nine."

I met with Mr. and Mrs. Woods at Newark Airport the next day. We drove to a restaurant, sat at a table, ordered a drink. The place was crowded. It was happy hour. Christopher handed me a paper bag.

"Do you want to count it?" he asked. "I can assure you, there's thirty thousand there."

I declined and gave him a slip of paper. "This is my phone number, Christopher. Call me only if an emergency arises—and don't say anything on the phone. I'll call you back from a pay phone immediately. Don't call me just to say hello, or to see how I'm doing, or to ask when I'm going to do this thing. I'll do it as soon as I can.

"And I want to warn the both of you: Forget all about this. Mum is the word. Don't talk to no one. Understand? Now I have to bring the money to the office, because they're the ones who'll take care of this. One more thing I forgot to tell you. You'll have to pay for expenses involved, not to exceed six thousand."

I was taking a shot. I don't know where I got these figures. But anyway it worked.

"No problem," Mrs. Woods said.

I grabbed a cab back to Newark Airport, then grabbed a different cab to Queens. I always covered myself in case I was wearing a tail.

I gave Little Dom $15,000, and we discussed the matter briefly.

"Joey, do the legwork and then I'll send Billy Ray down to do the job." Billy was part of Dominick's crew. "Put the guy in your Lincoln, they got big trunks. Drive to the 'Glades. Billy'll dig the

hole, because I know you don't want to get blisters. Just have everything ready, like the lime and everything, you know?"

I knew. We picked up a couple of hookers, had a few drinks, banged them. It cost $200 apiece. I flew back the next morning. My lovely wife greeted me at the airport.

"Honey, some guy called you last night and sounded annoyed that you weren't home." Bunny said. "Said he was Tommy's friend. Said Joe G."

Joe N. Gallo, the *consigliere*.

"I told him you'd be back today, Joe, and he said he'd call at three o'clock sharp and for you to be there. What's up?"

"Oh, that's Tommy's *compare*," I said. "I have to do him a favor. Will it ever stop?" I added, looking up to the sky and making a gesture like I was talking to God.

Break a Leg

Gallo called at exactly three o'clock and asked me if I remembered my conversation with Tommy several months before. Of course I remembered, the moron!

"Yes, sir," I answered. "I can have that room ready for you no later than tomorrow night. When is your niece going to return?"

"My niece will be returning Friday," he answered. This was a Wednesday, so I had to hurry. I really appreciated all the time he was giving me, the bastard. Luckily, I'd already done a little legwork, found Gallo's broad Sophia's brother's house in Naples, Florida, cased it, and spent a few days in the neighborhood. It had been a while since Tommy had told me in New York that Gallo wanted his girlfriend's brother messed up, and I thought he'd forgotten about it or changed his mind.

"Okay, Joe," I signed off. "Consider the job done."

I did like Tommy said. Drove to Miami that day. Got two spades. Told them what to do. Then I rented a car with a phony credit card and drove to the guy's house. I knocked on the door, and when Sophia's brother answered I made up a line about my rented car overheating. I knew he was a zip—that's what we call Italians from the other side—as he communicated in a fractured mixture of Italian and broken English.

"Whatsa matta? You car—shesa no good?"

My Italian was limited, but I could get by. The zip looked to be

in the late twenties, about five feet eight inches tall, and built real hard. The spades had their work cut out for them.

"Cumma in. The telephone, shesa inna kitchen."

After going through the charade of calling the car rental company, Sophia's brother offered me a glass of red wine, and we sat and talked. He began telling me about his "beautiful" sister, how she was in love with some old man who was a big shot in the Mafia, how much he disliked the bastard. "If I see him, I breaka his fuckin' head," he said.

His name was Alberto. Alberto poured me another glass of wine and we continued to talk. Broken English and broken Italian. He showed me a picture of Sophia. I had never seen such a beautiful Italian girl in my life. Jet black hair and black eyes. What the fuck was she doing with that old cocksucker Gallo? I wondered.

"Giovanni, another glassa wine?"

"Just one more, Alberto. The car people should be here soon."

I knew I was showing my face, a cardinal no-no in the leg-breaking business. But there was no way Alberto could connect me with the coming events. I lived too far away and never came to Naples anyway. Almost never.

Finally there came a knock at the door. Alberto rose to answer it, and it was the two spades. They asked him to use the phone, to call Hertz and let the office know they found me.

As Alberto was following one guy into the kitchen, the other dropped a canvas sack over his head and the upper part of his body. He was struggling and yelling in Italian for me to help. The other spade hit him on the head with a lead pipe and knocked him out. We tied his hands behind his back, lashed his ankles together, and threw him in my trunk.

I shot over to Alligator Alley and began the long drive to Fort Lauderdale on that dark, desolate road. I figured I'd drive about sixty miles before dumping him. I wanted to get off the Alley before he came to or was discovered.

When I found a nice dark pull-off, I stopped the car. Alberto was still unconscious. I told the spades to break one leg, smash the knuckles on his right hand, and blacken both eyes. It took them two minutes.

We left Alberto on the side of the road. I took the guys to Miami, gave them a grand, and returned the car. Then I went to the Diplomat for a drink. I was in the Tack Room when Tommy called.

"Your wife told me you'd probably be there," he said. "My *compare* called and told me that you told him you'd take care of that thing by tomorrow night."

"What thing?" I asked, acting stupid.

"You know what thing!" I could hear his aggravation building.

"Hey, Tommy, are you home or at a pay phone? If you're home, call it a 'thing.' But if you're at a pay phone, talk straight. Because I don't know what the fuck you're talking about. Tomorrow night, you say? I'm supposed to do something for your *compare?*"

I was really breaking his balls now. I could picture the flecks of foam spraying out of his mouth.

"Hey, Joey, remember when you came up to New York and you met— What the fuck are you laughing at?"

"Tell your *compare* it's done," I said. "I did it tonight. Would I be here if I didn't do it tonight?"

"*Marrone,* Joey, that was fast. Did you do it like I told you? You know, rent the thing and get the two eggplants and all?" He meant the black guys.

"No, T.A., I got two egg rolls instead," I answered. "It cost me over a G. I hope the old fuck appreciates it."

"Don't worry, Joey, he will. Let me call him now and tell him. He'll cum in his pants. Call me tomorrow." And he hung up.

I went home that night and called Dominick at the Casbah Lounge in Queens. I warned him not to tell Tommy about that deal we had going with the sixty large from the old Jersey couple.

The Double-Bang

A week after I took care of that job for the *consigliere,* Sean O'Leary called.

"Joe, it's the last week at Gulfstream, so let's get together this Saturday and do a good one."

I made arrangements to meet Sean at the track and decided to get to work on that Christopher Woods package. I found out where Joseph DeMarco worked, and I even stopped by the dealership pretending I wanted to buy a Buick. He was in the used-car department. I became a little friendly with him and we went out after my test drive for drinks.

He wanted me to stop by his place for a drink, as well as to meet his wife. I declined. I didn't want to meet her, as she could finger me as a new acquaintance of his in the event anything went wrong. I told him I'd let him know about the car.

He asked for my phone number, but I stalled him with a story about being in the process of moving. I told Joseph I'd call him when they connected my phone. He thought I was a vacuum cleaner salesman by the name of Joe Russo. That was the phony ID I was carrying at the time.

. . .

"Joey, that guy who says that his father is the New Jersey boss . . ."

"Yeah?"

"Well, his father is a guard at a New Jersey state prison. A working stiff. He's nothing. Not connected at all." It was Little Dom calling from New York.

"Okay," I told Dominick. "I never thought he was anybody. I'm almost set down here. I just have to pick up the lime. When are you sending Billy Ray down?"

"Whenever you want. He's ready. He can come this weekend if you want."

"Nah, wait until next week, after Gulfstream closes," I said. "I'm doing something for Tommy over there."

Dominick was interested. "What you got going, Joey? Can I get down?"

"Sorry, Dom. No sense getting in now. It'll be over in a few days and I can't go into details."

"Yeah, okay, Joey. Let me know when you want me to send Billy down." He hung up.

"Jesus Christ, Sean, couldn't you get a couple more jockeys? Boxing seven horses is going to cost us eighty-four bucks a ticket!"

It was a twelve-horse field and Sean had reached only five of the jocks. True, they were the five favorites, and Sean was sure we'd do real well boxing the longshots, but still. Seven horses?

"We can do real good here, Joey," Sean assured me. "How much money did you bring?"

"I'm carrying a hundred large," I told him.

"Good. Bet it all. You should have brought more. Now start betting early, it takes a long time to box seven horses. The three horse and the eight horse got speed. Gamble a little and wheel them a couple a hundred times on top of the box."

What could I do? There was something about the whole thing I didn't like, including the fact that Sean had "fixed" a new jockey. But he assured me this jockey had pulled for him before in Califor-

nia and told me to quit worrying and start betting. When I met with Freddie he almost had a heart attack when I told him what we were doing.

"Seven horses!" Freddie blurted. "What, is he crazy? What the fuck are we gonna make?"

"Well, he claims we'll do good because they're all longshots and because of the big handle the last Saturday of the meet brings in."

"And who the fuck is this new jockey?" asked Freddie, not mollified in the least. "He was never in our fix before. I don't like it, Joe. I think somebody got to Sean. I'd like to pass on it."

"Yeah, me, too," I told Freddie. "But what if we pass and it comes back big? What do we tell Al Capone up in New York? You know he's not going to believe us."

"Yeah, I guess we better go after it," Freddie said.

"Here's your half," I said, handing him fifty large. "Use the balance on the box but save some for wheels on the three horse and eight horse. Sean said they both got speed. And start betting early. Seven horses take a while to box."

Post time. The race was a six-furlong event. That's three quarters of a mile. The rider we were suspicious about was aboard a four-to-one shot, the third choice on the board. He won by eight lengths. We lost $100,000.

I met up with Freddie, and we both wanted to puke. We couldn't go after the jockey, so we went looking for Sean.

We found him behind the barns, and I backhanded him to the face. He reeled backward about ten feet, fell to the ground, and when he got up I hit him again.

"Be at the Diplomat Wednesday," I told him quietly. That's when T.A. would be down. I was about to smack Sean again when Matty Brown Fortunato, the Genovese capo, appeared out of the blue. Matty Brown's turf was Calder, not Gulfstream. Freddie and I just looked at each other knowingly.

"Fuck it, we got double-banged," I told him on the way out. "Let Tommy take care of it."

. . .

Murphy's law. Everything was going down the tubes. Not only did we lose a hundred grand but I got a speeding ticket driving home from the track. I called the cop a cocksucker, and he pinched me. Bunny had to bail me out for a G-note. To make matters worse, the next afternoon I got a call from Christopher Woods in New Jersey.

"Joe, please call me" was all he said.

When I reached him from a pay phone he told me his daughter was going away with her husband. Joseph and Carolyn were taking a two-month European vacation.

"Christopher, call up your Joseph and Carolyn, get them on two different extensions, and tell them this: Tell them that your wife has been sick and that she plans to leave Carolyn half a million in her will. Tell them that in the event Carolyn isn't around to collect, the money goes to your grandchild on her thirty-fifth birthday. I guarantee you, Christopher, that gold digger will treat Carolyn like a queen on their European trip. In fact, I'm surprised the dirtbag hasn't shaken down your wife already."

"Oh, he has," Christopher said. "He made us buy a new car, paid for in Carolyn's name. He drives around in it now. He said if we didn't, we could never visit our grandchild again. We feel like we got away cheap. But we expect him to come back for more."

I couldn't help wondering exactly how much money these people were worth. But this was beyond bazookas now. After listening to Christopher's story, I couldn't wait to whack that cocksucker DeMarco myself.

"Okay, Christopher, we have to wait, that's all. Our deal still stands. In the meantime, don't mention anything about me to Carolyn. And don't worry about her returning from her trip. With half a million dollars awaiting her return, Joseph will be carrying her down the gangplank like they were newlyweds."

"Straighten Joe Dogs Out!"

"Look, Tom, we were fucked by Sean and that's all there is to it," I said into the pay phone. "It's no coincidence that the Calder outfit from Kansas City suddenly shows up at Gulfstream and we lose a hundred large. And Freddie is pissed off. He wants his end. Now."

"Fuck Freddie," Tommy growled. "How much we got left?"

"About a hundred grand."

"Yeah? Well, bring that with you Wednesday to the Dip, Joey. Is Sean going to be there?"

"Six o'clock sharp. I told him the Tack Room."

"Okay," Tommy said. "We'll straighten this out then. And, oh, by the way, I have a message for you from my *compare*," he added. And then he hung up.

I called Little Dom and told him to hold off on sending Billy Ray south.

"Gee, Joey," he complained, "I was counting on that extra bread. I took a bath at the track. But maybe that's how these things happen. Who knows? Maybe it's for the best. Maybe they'll change their minds. Maybe they'll forget about the whole thing."

"Yeah, maybe," I said.

. . .

I was sitting with Tommy in the Tack Room of the Diplomat that Wednesday when Sean O'Leary walked in with Matty Brown Fortunato. We all discussed what happened, Sean's story being that the jockey double-banged us. Then Sean complained about me smacking him around.

Matty Brown took Sean's side on the beating—if you could call it a beating—and wanted Tommy to do something about it, or else he would take it further himself.

"Tommy, I'm only showing you this respect and consideration because I've known you for a long time and you're close to Joe G.," Matty Brown said. "So show me the respect and straighten Joe Dogs out."

Tommy replied, "First of all, Matty, in all due respect, this Irish cocksucker fucked us out of one hundred large. You're the one who's intervening on this thing and, I might add, going against your own people. As far as taking this any further, you can do what you want. But it's on record that Sean is with me.

"And I'm telling you up front, Matty, that I will take this right to the top. And let me go even further. It was me who told Joe Dogs to kick the shit out of Sean if this ever happened. Sean got away easy, because I was going to rip his fuckin' eyes out. I'll show you the respect and not touch him. But I do expect you to straighten him out."

Matty looked at Sean and smacked him and said that he hadn't known what this whole thing was about. He wasn't aware, he said, that we'd lost so much money. Then he asked Tommy to promise not to harm Sean.

Tommy declined, saying, "I can't promise you that. I have to see first what my *compare* has to say."

Matty Brown and Tommy A. shook hands, and Matty and Sean walked out the door.

"Tommy, they just gave us the nicest hand job that I ever had," I said.

"Yeah, Joey, I know. I came in my pants, too. But there's nothing

I can do about it. Matty Brown's a capo. Let my *compare* handle it. It's a good thing I cut him in."

"Well, Tom, I'm glad you did, too. So what do you say, how about I give Freddie the hundred grand we got left?"

"Joey, you give me the money, and tell Freddie to come see me. I'll give him something. You listening to what I'm saying?"

"Yeah, Tom, I hear you. I'll tell him. Do whatever you want. I'll bring you the money tomorrow—unless somebody robs it." I smiled.

"Hey, Joey, they steal the money, they better steal you with it."

The next day I delivered Tommy's one hundred large, and told him I'd pass on his message to Freddie.

"Wait until next week, Joey. I'll be back in New York. You tell him what to do. But don't tell him how. Let's see if Freddie knows how to reach out."

Tommy A. was testing Freddie. He wanted to see just how much pull he had outside of Florida. Ten days later I delivered Tommy's message.

"But what about what Sean did?" Freddie wanted to know. "Isn't Tommy going to make good on that money we lost?"

"Freddie, I don't know what he's doing. You ask him. It's out of my hands. I was told to mind my own business, and that's what I'm doing. I'm just delivering a message from Tommy. He has your money."

"God Will Punish All of Us"

I was delivering a lot of messages for Tommy around then. Gradually, over four years, I'd leapfrogged Skinny Bobby DeSimone and become T.A.'s top guy in Florida. I think it was because of a combination of Tommy's lessons in Mafia attitude and my own ability to think quick on my feet. I never thought about if what I was doing was *right*, or *wrong*. My only concern was whether it was good for us. That's why I was able to take a case like Christopher Woods's.

Nearly three months went by before I heard from Woods, the good Christian from New Jersey who wanted his son-in-law whacked. He called in the summer of '76. Sean O'Leary's double-bang was fading to a bad memory.

"Joe, they're back," Christopher Woods breathed into the phone. "Your plan worked beautifully. Carolyn said Joseph treated her like a queen. And all he could talk about was what they were going to do with the money when my wife passed away. Can you believe the audacity of this guy? Carolyn said he made her sick, and

she couldn't wait to get home, because now she has enough courage to leave him. They're back home in Florida, have been for ten days."

"Christopher, don't call me, I'll call you—unless it's an emergency, of course."

I rented a car and did some surveillance. The thought occurred to me, not for the first time, that I should have been a cop. I wore this goofy fishing hat, and sunglasses, and I followed Joseph and Carolyn and their daughter on a Sunday when they went to the park. Carolyn was about five feet six, lovely figure, and extremely beautiful. She had soft, reddish-blond hair, the same as her daughter.

What a jerk this dumb wop was! Here he had a million-dollar family, in both senses of the phrase, and he was fucking it all up because of his greed.

And to tell you the truth, they did look like the perfect family. Carolyn walked with a slight limp, nearly imperceptible, but Joseph took her arm and helped her in and out of their car. He looked like the perfect husband, and I began to wonder if Christopher Woods was lying. I didn't know anything about these people except what Christopher told me.

Hey, Joe, I told myself, don't start making judgments. Just do what you're supposed to do, and collect the rest of the money. That's where my Mafia training came in handy.

Nonetheless, when I called Dominick and told him to send down Billy Ray, I mentioned my second thoughts.

"Joey, maybe the guy's being nice to her because of that half-million," Dominick said. "This is some story you're concocting. You should have been a screenplay writer. I'll send Billy down, and don't take a year doing this thing."

Two weeks later Billy Ray flew into town, and I booked him a room at the Holiday Inn in West Palm. We made plans to case Joseph's dealership the following day, and I told him to stay out of trouble.

"No problem, Joe, whatever you say. You have everything?" he asked. "Like a piece and all?"

"Yeah, yeah, Billy, I got everything. Including a pick and shovel."

. . .

The next morning Bunny was in my ear. "Joe, wake up! Some guy named Christopher wants you on the phone. He says it's an emergency."

I left the house and called Christopher Woods from a pay phone.

"Joe, you didn't do it yet, did you?"

"Hey, Christopher, I told you not to break my balls about this thing." I felt like calling the whole deal off. "What the fuck are you calling me for? It's in the process right now."

"That's why I'm calling, Joe. Please, please stop it. We beg of you. My wife and I will never be able to live with it. We'll take our daughter away from Joseph, and we'll have the law take care of him. Keep the money we gave you, only don't harm him."

I didn't believe what I was hearing. Sure, I could stop it. But after all the rigmarole with the setup, what with Billy Ray traveling down and all, I wanted to go through with it if for nothing else than the laid-out expenses.

I gathered my thoughts. And lied. "First of all, Christopher, I don't even know if I *can* stop it now. Number two, the office is expecting the balance of the money by tomorrow, plus expenses. Number three, I'll have to go crazy hunting down the guy the office sent to actually do the job. And number four, I have to call the office to get their permission to stop it."

"Joe, please," Christopher begged. "I'll give you the balance of the money tomorrow, or even today. If you do this to Joseph, God will punish all of us. Call your office and tell your people we'll come up with the balance, plus all expenses. Please call them, Joe, and call me right back."

"Hey, Billy, wake up, you punchy fuck," I said into the pay phone. "It's cancelled. But I want you to stay a few days. I'll clear it with Dominick. I'll pick you up in an hour."

I went to have coffee, and then called Little Dom, explaining Christopher Woods's sudden change of heart.

"We might be better off this way, as long as we're still getting

the money," Dominick said. "I didn't like the idea of so many people knowing who you were, anyway. I'm surprised, though, that they're still paying off the balance. Here's what you do, Joey. Let Billy keep five G's, take it out of my end, and keep him there, if you want, for another week."

I called Christopher and told him that I'd managed to call it off in time, that the office understood, but unfortunately he'd still have to come up with the $30,000.

"God bless you, Joe, God bless you. Fly in tomorrow, we'll pick you up at the airport and have the money. Or if you want, my wife and I will fly down to you, so it won't be an inconvenience."

My God, what nice people this family was. I couldn't just let it go at that. So naturally I came up with a plan.

"Christopher," I said, "you fly in Monday, and check into that Howard Johnson's near your daughter's. What time does your grandchild get out of school?"

"Three o'clock. Why?" he asked.

"Never mind why, just call me at noon Monday, from the Howard Johnson's at Deerfield Beach. Don't bring any money with you. Maybe we can cut through all this nonsense without anyone getting hurt."

"We'll fly in Sunday," he said. "And I'll call you on Monday."

"Okay, Christopher," I said. "And don't let Carolyn know you're coming down."

Over the weekend, I told Billy what I had in mind. "I don't think you should show your face to them," I said. "You never know what could happen down the line."

Billy agreed.

At 1:30 P.M. on Monday, I met with Christopher and his wife at the Howard Johnson's. There were just a few things I had to get straight in my mind.

"Christopher, do you actually know that your daughter wants to leave her husband?" I asked. "She's willing to take her kid and come back to New Jersey with you?"

"Joe, to be perfectly honest with you, I don't actually know," he answered. "She's mentioned leaving him. She's told us how unhappy she is. Carolyn said she was sad and sorry six months after

their marriage. She's told us he beats her, but we've never seen the bruises. But then again, we do live over one thousand miles away. I can't imagine, however, that Carolyn has been lying to us. We are, or were, a very close family. But I don't even know how Carolyn would feel if we went there right now unannounced."

"Okay, listen, Christopher. Here's what I have in mind," I said. "At three o'clock this afternoon the three of us will go to your daughter's apartment. You will call her first, tell her you're here, and explain that you'll be right over. I'll drive you there, and in front of me, we will ask Carolyn if she wants to leave Joseph.

"I have two men parked in a moving van on her block right now. If she says yes, the men will load all her furniture and take it anywhere you want, even to New Jersey. Now don't worry about Joseph. No one will get hurt unless they ask for it. And I don't want any money for this. It's a gift."

"God bless you, Joe," Mr. and Mrs. Woods said in unison.

At three o'clock, Christopher dialed his daughter. "Hello, Carrot Top, Mumsie and I are at the Howard Johnson's. . . . That's right, around the corner. . . . Honest. . . . Yes, we're coming over."

I'm looking at Christopher, and I gave him a gesture to hurry it up and make it short while I'm ushering his wife out the door. They jumped in my car, and as we were leaving I saw Billy Ray pulling into the Howard Johnson's parking lot, just as we planned.

Within thirty seconds we were in front of the duplex, and Carolyn was already waiting at the curb. She had a black eye. As I got out, the two big lobs from my crew left the moving van and began walking up the street to meet me.

"Who are you?" Carolyn asked me, shooting her parents a concerned look.

"I'm a friend of your mother and father," I answered. "And we don't have much time. Do you want to leave your husband?"

Carolyn was obviously confused. She looked from me to her parents, who were both nodding as if to say, Yes, it's true, and then she burst into tears and ran into her parents' arms.

"Oh, Mama," she sobbed like a little girl, "I've been waiting so

long for you and Daddy to come and get me and take me and the baby away from this nightmare. Thank God it's finally over."

I broke up the happy reunion and told my boys to get started, with Carolyn eventually pointing out what she wanted them to load. She left most of the furniture and packed only clothes. And on the short drive back to the Howard Johnson's I assured her that she would be safe from Joseph.

"What happened to your eye?" Christopher Woods asked his daughter, but Carolyn looked too embarrassed to say anything in front of me or her daughter, whom she was now cradling in her arms.

I didn't have time for explanations, at any rate, as I saw Billy Ray sitting in his rental car and pointing to his watch. It was now three-thirty.

"Look, Christopher," I said. "I have a lot to do. This thing isn't completely solved yet. Take a cab to the airport at West Palm Beach and get back to New Jersey. I'll call you late tonight, around midnight, maybe later. I have to go now."

I reached our rendezvous before Billy and quickly changed the license plates on my car. I lit a cigarette and waited. Fifteen minutes later Billy and Joseph pulled up in a powder blue Oldsmobile.

As I approached their car, I noticed that Billy had pulled a gun and was pressing it into Joseph DeMarco's ear. I walked up, opened the passenger-side door, and ordered Joseph into the back seat. Billy climbed in next to him. He was limp, begging for his life. He had no idea what was happening. He did, however, recognize me as Joe Russo.

"What's wrong?" he stuttered. "Joe, what did I do? Why are you doing this to me?"

"Billy," I barked, "shove the gun in his mouth and let him suck on the muzzle. I don't want to be disturbed while I talk to this cocksucker."

I drove to a secluded parking lot and pulled into the back next to a fence. I clicked off the ignition and turned in my seat. "Joseph, I'm going to tell you this one time, and I want you to pay attention.

I don't want to hear one word from you. Billy, take the piece out of his mouth. If he says one fuckin' word while I'm talking, hit him in the eye with the gun. Is that what you used on Carolyn, you motherfucker?"

I wanted to kill the guy. I wanted to cut his balls off. But I had to be a professional now.

"Joseph, your wife left you," I said. "I'm even going to tell you where she is. Because I'm sure by the time we're through here, you're going to do as I say. She went to her mother's house in Ridgewood, New Jersey—Carolyn and her child, who I am going to adopt after Carolyn divorces you and we get married. Joseph, I'm not going to kill you here today. But I—"

"You don't know who the fuck you're talking to," he blurted out. I gave Billy a nod. "My father—"

Billy smacked him in the eye and over the bridge of his nose with his forty-five. He opened a gash from Joseph's eyebrow to his nose. I threw him a towel.

"Open your fuckin' mouth again while I'm talking and the other eye gets it," I said. "Now, you were mentioning your father. Joseph, listen to me. This is where your father works."

I told him the prison, and Joseph's good eye went wide. Then I handed him a slip of paper with an address. "And this is where your father lives with your mother."

All the color drained from Joseph's face. He slumped back in the seat.

"Now, Joseph, if you don't do what I tell you, I'll kill your father. I won't kill you, but I'll maim you. And you will have to live with the fact that you got your father killed. We will even let your mother live, but let her know the reason her husband got killed.

"Now, you wouldn't want that to happen, would you? Don't answer. Just nod yes or no."

He shook his head back and forth.

"Now, Joseph, you know we could kill you now. But I'm going to give you a chance. One month from today, you will call Carolyn and see if she still feels the same way about having left you. Other than that one call, you will have no contact with her. She'll be with me most of the time, and she knows how to reach me. In the event

that something happens to her, her daughter, or her parents, your father will be killed within the hour.

"If you want to know how well I know Carolyn, she has a birthmark on the right cheek of her ass and a scar on the inside of her thigh just below her pussy."

I'd gotten this information from Christopher and his wife.

"Carolyn and I see each other while you're working, you jackoff. Every time I fly in from New York, we get together. This has been going on for six months. She doesn't love you at all, you fuckin' moron. She just doesn't want you killed, and I'm only letting you live because I made her a promise. But, Joseph, I could break that promise. Do you understand?"

Joseph DeMarco nodded his head vigorously as I started Billy's car.

I drove back to our rendezvous and told Billy to open the trunk of the Olds. Joseph went white again, and his body went stiff. But I was only looking to see if the car had a spare tire and jack. It did. I took the gun from Billy and shot out a front tire.

"Okay, Joseph," I said. "Change the tire. And when you get back, tell your boss the jack slipped and hit you in the eye. Billy, let's go."

Billy was a chatterbox on the drive back to West Palm. "Joe, that was so sweet and beautiful, I can't wait to tell Dominick. I know you really wanted to whack that guy. His wife is a baby doll, even with the shiner."

"They're a nice family, Billy, well educated and all," I said. "She just got tied up with a moron who didn't know how to handle a wife and family. He could have milked them for the rest of his life if he had any brains."

"Here, Joe," Billy said, "here's your five large. All you have to do is pick up my hotel bill. Dominick paid for the plane tickets."

"No, Billy, that's yours," I said. "Dominick knew what was coming down, and he said to let you keep it. He'll straighten it out with me later. And here's another three grand from me. I know you didn't have to do anything, but you were here if I needed you. Let's stop at my house and have a drink before we go out."

He Loved Her So Much He Killed Her

Billy Ray was pretty typical of the kind of fellows who became mobsters, the type of person I was now calling "colleagues." He might not have been the toughest guy who ever came down the block, or the smartest, or the shrewdest. But, Jesus Christ, he was one of the craziest. I mean, not ha-ha crazy, but kill-your-wife insane. Even for my taste, and I was pretty nuts. I remember him telling me a story, right after the Joseph DeMarco bang-up, that still has my head shaking. It was about how he'd been "forced" into the unpleasant position of having to murder his lovely wife.

The two of us had barely walked through my front door after scaring the shit out of DeMarco before Bunny was on me like a fuckin' Ban-Lon shirt. "Joe, a Tony Esposito has been trying to reach you. He said he's been waiting in Deerfield Beach for three hours. He wanted to know what to do with the load of clothes you ordered moved. So I told him to drive to West Palm and check into the Holiday Inn. Here's his room number. Joe, what's he talking about?"

"Tony? Tony? Oh fuck!" I said, remembering the moving van with Carolyn's wardrobe. "I'd completely forgotten about him. You did the right thing, Bunny, telling him to come here. Thanks."

"And you got another call," she continued. "Guy named Christopher called and said for you to deliver Carolyn's stuff to the house in New Jersey.

"Who's Christopher?" Bunny asked. "And, more important, who's Carolyn?"

I had to hand it to Bunny, she didn't miss a trick. I really loved her. I explained that I'd done a piece of work for a guy named Christopher and his daughter, and that Tony—who was Louie Esposito's son, by the way—was delivering a truckload of stuff to New Jersey.

I met Tony, bought him breakfast, threw him a G, gave him the Woods's address in Ridgewood, New Jersey, and sent him on his way. Then I told Billy that before I put him on a plane I needed him for one more job. "We have to see a lawyer named Thomas Roberts."

During the ride to Roberts's place in Boca Raton, Billy started musing on the crazy relationships between men and women. He told me he understood how much I loved Bunny, but he also sensed how much I wanted to bang that baby doll Carolyn. Billy was on intimate terms with such matters of the heart, he explained. He'd been in love once, too.

A few years back, he said, he'd married his childhood sweetheart. Their honeymoon was interrupted when Billy had to go in for an eighteen-month stretch for assault.

"When I came home, I found out she was fucking one of my so-called friends. From the first day I went into the can! I couldn't believe it. I wouldn't believe it. I told her I had to go to California on a piece of work. I told her I'd be gone for a week, maybe ten days, but that I'd call her every night. When I called her that night from Los Angeles and told her I loved her, she said to me, 'Ditto.' Ditto, Joe, can you fucking believe it? I knew he was there in the bed," Billy said, beating his fists into his thighs for emphasis.

So Billy picked up a hooker and banged her for $200. The next day he made arrangements with the hooker to stay in his hotel

room and for $500 to play a role in what he told her was a practical joke. Billy gave the hooker his home telephone number and asked her to call his house—collect from Billy—at midnight eastern time. Then he hopped a flight back to New York under an assumed name and picked up a forty-five with a silencer.

"I got to my house at about eleven-twenty P.M., parked a block away, and opened the front door with my key," Billy explained. "I heard a bunch of rumbling around in the bedroom. I walked in, flipped the light switch, and there they were, trying to get dressed. I shot him twice in the head and once in the heart.

"She was so scared she couldn't speak. Believe me, Joe, I didn't want to kill her. I loved her so much. If she would have fucked around with some stranger, I'd probably still be with her. But my close friend! I let her have the other three bullets in the head. Then I turned off all the lights and poured myself a drink. At midnight the phone rang. The operator said, 'Collect call to anyone from Billy,' and I accepted.

"I disguised my voice like a broad's for a few minutes, hung up, turned on the lights, put the television on loud, and flew back to California that night.

"Joe, I had the perfect alibi. They checked it out with the airlines, the hotel, the phone company. Everyone that knows me knows that I did it. Even the law knows. But go ahead, prove it. They can't. Joe, if it happened to you, I know you'd do the same. I had to do it to save face."

"I don't think so, Billy," I answered. "I'm no analyst, but I don't think I could ever kill Bunny if I caught her with anyone. To you, face-saving meant more than your love for your wife. That's not the way I am."

I stopped to call Thomas Roberts, and told him I had good news. He was so excited when I said I had something to give him that he invited me to his home. I warned Billy to keep an eye on Roberts's wife, Sarah. I had asked around and found that she was known for carrying a little twenty-five caliber in her purse. They said she wasn't shy about using it.

When I introduced Billy to the Robertses at their front door, Sarah was carrying her purse. Billy noticed.

"Let's all go into the living room for a drink," the lawyer suggested. Sarah sat on a love seat and I sat on a large sofa. Billy sat down next to Sarah. Thomas brought over a round of drinks and I offered a toast. Then I told the lawyer, "Thomas, I made a mistake over the phone when I said I had something to give you. You won't get anything from me."

"I don't understand," Sarah Roberts interrupted. "Why won't you give it to him? You must have earned a lot of money from our Woods family connection. At least we deserve some."

"Well, it wasn't money that I was going to give to your husband," I told Sarah. "I was going to give him a few smacks in the mouth. And if you want one of them, I'll be happy to oblige. Since you're talking like such a tough fucking guy, I'll be happy to treat you like one."

Sarah reached to unzip her purse, but Billy Ray backhanded her, nearly knocking her head off. He grabbed her pistol and began walking toward Thomas.

"Nah, Billy," I said, stepping between them. "Let him go, he's a cunt. He squats to piss. You've already smacked the man of this house."

I turned to Sarah. "Before I leave, lady, remember this: If you decide to call the law, don't forget to tell them that you hired me as a hit man to commit murder and that you were going to profit from it."

We left their house feeling good. "Hey, Billy," I asked on the way to the airport, "do you always smack broads like that?"

Two days later I wound up my business with Christopher Woods and family. He and his wife picked me up at Newark Airport. I was a little disappointed that Carolyn wasn't with them, but fairy tales don't come true. Once in their car, Christopher passed back a bag containing $30,000. They had offered me the front passenger side but I don't sit there with strangers, as that is the seat where a lot of people get whacked.

The Woodses even offered me expense money, but in all good conscience I had to decline. "The only other thing you owe me is a

Dewar's Scotch on the rocks," I told them as we headed for a restaurant near the airport.

Carolyn was waiting for us when we got there, and I proceeded to relate to all three the tale of Joseph DeMarco's scary little test drive. I left out the part about Billy cracking Joseph with the gun, although I did mention that I had given her former husband a payback black eye. Carolyn hugged me and kissed me—I had warned her parents not to mention that I'd been paid for this job —and I felt great, if a little out of place drinking with ordinary "citizens." After dinner I called Dominick from the restaurant and told him to meet me at Newark Airport for his share.

"In the event Joseph calls before the month is up, get in touch with me right away," I told Carolyn before we parted. "In fact, Carolyn, you can call anytime."

I meet Little Dom at midnight, one hour before boarding, and flew back first class drinking double Dewar's all the way. Sometimes you run into situations where the law just can't cut it. This had been one. The Woodses had no choice but to seek help for their problem from someone like me. So it cost them sixty grand? So what? They did it to save their daughter. They would have paid double that price if necessary.

Bunny was surprised to see me come home. She was punchy from sleep—it was early in the morning—but not sleepy enough to hold back a crack. "What's wrong, honey?" she asked. "Don't you like to fuck in New Jersey?"

"Go back to sleep, Bunny. I had a rough day and I don't want no bullshit. I just left some nice people, not like you and I. Nice people, and a lady. Now shut the fuck up."

January 19, 1981. The FBI showed me this photo of myself just before I went to my first trial in 1984. It brought back memories of how mad I was. The photo encouraged me throughout the first trial in which I spent a total of twenty-eight days on the stand.

Outside of undercover club at 100 Broadway, Riviera Beach, Florida.

Downstairs at Suite 100. Picture of Bette Davis on wall. (*Photo by Howard Loth.*)

Upstairs at Suite 100.

DATE DUE